HOUSE
MATES

HOUSE MATES

A PRACTICAL GUIDE TO LIVING WITH OTHER PEOPLE

Teona Tone
and Deanna Sclar

FAWCETT COLUMBINE · NEW YORK

A Fawcett Columbine Book
Published by Ballantine Books

Published in the United States by Ballantine Books,
a division of Random House, Inc., New York,
and simultaneously in Canada
by Random House of Canada Limited, Toronto.

Cover design by Richard Rossiter
Text design by Amy Lamb

Library of Congress Catalog Card Number: 84-90836
ISBN 0-449-90110-6

Manufactured in the United States of America

FIRST EDITION: MARCH 1985

10 9 8 7 6 5 4 3 2 1

To all those we've ever shared a home with
and to all those who've ever tried to split
three rooms four ways.

ANNOTATED TABLE OF CONTENTS

hold and why they usually find the results more than worth the effort!

This chapter will tell you how to find just the right people to live with. Before you start looking for a roommate, it is important to figure out just whom you are looking for. We provide a large selection of questions to ask yourself in order to get your personal tastes and priorities in order—not only whether or not someone smokes, or is into drugs or liquor (who wants to drink alone?) but whether he or she feels comfortable with kids, pets, and your favorite kind of music. Next, we get into how and where to advertise for someone to live with. We present the traditional options, plus a few gimmicks you might never think of. It's important to use a preliminary telephone interview to screen prospective applicants or landlords. We've furnished telephone checklists for both rentees and renters to keep you from missing any important points. Then we discuss and demystify the daunting prospect of interviewing strangers face to face and stress the need to trust your intuition while getting all the facts. Finally we tell you how to check personal and financial references to be sure that the people you select are compatible and trustworthy. The accent is on reliable, practical ways to evaluate yourself and other people as potential housemates.

It is vitally important to agree on how the household will run and how the responsibilities and work will be divided *before* starting to live together. We deal with such issues as how the rent, mortgage, household insurance, utilities, and other monthly expenses will be split; how telephone messages will be taken and delivered; how the household chores and yard work will be divided; who will care for pets and plants (not to mention children!); whose furniture will go where; how storage areas will be divided; what the parking arrangements will be; and a host of other minor details that can turn into major problems if they aren't worked out beforehand. We provide lists of things to consider and show you how others have dealt with some of these questions. The accent is on getting everything done with a minimum of hassle.

Safety experts say that the kitchen is the most dangerous room in the house. This goes *double* in group households! We talk about shared cooking arrangements, cooking separately, how to organize the refrigerator and the cupboards, and how to keep the kitchen clean without one person doing all the work. We show you how to deal with food hogs who eat more than their share or pilfer other people's groceries, and how to create relaxed and pleasant mealtimes instead of the pandemonium that can occur when exhausted adults and overactive kids meet at the dinner table at the end of the day. What all this adds up to is how to turn a kitchen full of strangers into a center of goodwill and cooperation.

Any shared household that includes single people will inevitably find lovers and guests in its midst. Whether they just stay over occasionally or turn into permanent housemates, they do have an effect on the rest of the household. Next to conflicts over the kitchen, conflicts over the presence of "outsiders" is the greatest problem in most shared living situations. We've found that it really doesn't matter what kind of rules you set up, as long as everyone agrees and is comfortable with them. We talk about the effect on the children in the household (which is never as traumatic as the effect on their parents!) and the need for housemates to be as open as possible about their feelings on the subject. We deal with a number of potential problems, such as guests who unwittingly break the house rules, invasion of privacy, and noisy lovemaking. We tell a couple of stories and provide guidelines for keeping a group household agreeing that "All the world loves a lover!"

Chapter VI. "All I Want Is a Little Peace and Quiet!" · 138

How to deal with the single factor that makes most people reluctant to share living space with others: the fear that their privacy will be invaded. Everyone needs some quiet time alone to relax undisturbed—to read, to meditate, or simply to doze off. People who study or work at home are particularly vulnerable on this point (especially those of us who are addicted to long baths or who do most of our best thinking on the john!). We've learned that pets can be as jealous as little children and find amazingly creative ways to express their feelings. We make suggestions about how to identify and satisfy your individual needs for peace and privacy and how to become sensitive to the unique needs of your housemates.

Chapter VII. "She's Not My Sister, We Just Live Together": Living with Your Own Kids or with Other People's Children · 147

If living with your own kids can be difficult, living with someone else's can be even worse. Or it can mean happiness, growth, and harmony for everyone in the house! We talk about the unique rewards and drawbacks of living with other people's children, and offer reasons why single people should seriously consider looking for a group household that includes them. We also explore the surprising fact that, for single parents, living with even *more* kids can make caring for their own much easier. We discuss the adjustment problems the children may encounter: crushes on older housemates, jealousy among "surrogate siblings," the tendency to play off one adult against the other, the refusal to obey a housemate because "You're not my parent," juvenile sexual experimentation, and other potentially thorny issues. You'll love the story about how a teenage only child found new enthusiasm for living as the "big brother" in an extended family!

Chapter VIII. A Family of Friends · 173

Turning a houseful of strangers into a family of friends can require tact and diplomacy, especially when disagreements occur. We turn you on to some basic techniques for avoiding friction in your household and show you what to do if it occurs. The most vital elements in maintaining good relationships with roommates is the establishment of a firm, written agreement up front and a weekly family meeting to talk over changes, deal with disputes, and let each other know what's happening in your lives.

Chapter IX. Staying on the Right Side of the Law · 186

Would you like to start group housekeeping in the home you currently own or rent? Then you'd better know how many unrelated people or families are allowed to share space in your area! Are you considering converting the garage or other extra space into an apartment or renting out the guest house? Then you'd better know how to deal with zoning regulations, building permits, and site modifications. Is it legal to sublet the space you currently rent? What are your rights as a landlord? As a tenant? And what are your liabilities? These are only a few of the things you must know if you are planning to buy, build, or rent a house, apartment, or condominium with one or more others. Local ordinances and laws vary, and it usually isn't too difficult to find out what the rules of the game are—if you know whom to ask! We provide lots of advice and informtion on dealing with the administrative mind, getting the basic agreements down in writing, and choosing insurance; and we illustrate some of the legal pitfalls and unexpected rewards of group housekeeping. Recommended reading for real estate and rental agents, no matter whom they live with!

Chapter X. "So Long. It's Been Good to Know You!" · 206

Even the most harmonious group households eventually lose a member or split up entirely. Whether it's a happy event like getting married, an unavoidable circumstance like a move to another town, or an irreconcilable personality conflict, the dissolution of a group living arrangement can be fairly thorny if you haven't set up things properly beforehand. For instance, whose plants are they if you bought them for next to nothing when they were seedlings and everyone in the household has shared the work of nurturing them into small trees? And if you've all contributed to buying a new set of pots, does someone who's leaving take one along, get reimbursed by the household, or just consider the contribution more than compensated by the years of using *all* the pots? We prescribe a lot of preventive medicine and offer suggestions on handling last-minute conflicts.

INTRODUCTION:

Creative Alternatives to Living Alone

Back in the "good old days" (at least ten years ago), the Great American Dream was not considered a fantasy. People actually did grow up in nice, roomy houses; go to school; get married; and raise kids in nice, roomy houses of their own. Those who eschewed the "white picket-fence route" were usually able to establish themselves in apartments that, generally speaking, held one family at a time. The most exotic living arrangements most of us ever encountered involved two or three single people—invariably of the same sex—sharing an apartment together. Any deviation from these situations was considered kinky. Most people thought shared living arrangements were undertaken only by long-haired "freaks" who gathered together in communes because their ideas and life-styles were too far-out for their "straight" families to handle, or by idealists who were trying out utopian experiments that always seemed to revolve around Eastern religions and unpalatable health foods. What's more, if two people of the same sex lived alone together for too long, others began to wonder whether "something was going on" between them.

Today we have many more options and people are free to find creative ways to arrange their living situations to suit themselves.

We have written this book for everyone who is struggling to make ends meet in this increasingly difficult economy. And for all those single parents who are trying valiantly to be mother, father, housekeeper, wage earner, cook, chauffeur, gardener, and playmate simultaneously. (Surely single parenthood is the twentieth century's most wryly humorous version of the one-man band!) In fact, this book is written for *everybody* who just doesn't want to live alone.

Let's take a closer look at some of the reasons that have prompted people to set up group households:

Because of the skyrocketing cost of housing, many young couples can no longer expect to buy—or even to rent—a house of their own even if both of them work full time. The median cost of a new home in California is currently $125,000 and climbing. Interest rates have gone as high as 20 percent and may again reach that level. Faced with mortgage payments that can be as high as $2,000 per month; plus property taxes and insurance; plus the increased costs of food, clothing, gasoline, and utilities, even many two-income couples can't afford to buy a house. Yet houses are better investments than ever and most people would still love to own one. Many have gone ahead and made the leap only to find that they cannot make the payments. In some cases, the easiest solution to this problem has been to rent the spare bedroom or to convert the garage (sometimes illegally) into an income-producing apartment. Some couples have formed partnerships with other married or single people and bought or rented a house together.

The climbing divorce rate has done almost as much to encourage shared housing arrangements as the high price of real estate. Many divorced mothers (or fathers) are given custody of a large house in the suburbs along with the kids—often a house one adult could not possibly maintain alone even without having to work to support a family. Other divorced parents do not want their children cooped up in apartments or cannot find apartments that will accept children. At the same time, they cannot afford to buy or rent a house where the kids can have a yard to play in.

One solution has been for two such single-parent families to join forces and move in together. The result can be bliss—or it can be utter chaos and confusion, with everyone's kids competing to see who can wreak the most havoc. As veterans of both situations, we've learned that the major pitfalls can usually be avoided by taking some care in selecting housemates and reaching agreement beforehand on the guidelines you'll follow in your household.

Other single-parent families have chosen to share housing with one or more single adults without children. For the single parent, having another adult around to help cope with junior after a hard day's work can be invaluable. The added stability of having another adult or adults in the house can often make the difference between a lost, bewildered child and a happy, secure one. A housemate who is not directly responsible for a child's welfare and support can often be both more objective and more loving. Some exceptional housemates not only provide strong role models, but may even act as surrogate parents. Shared housing can be used to create an extended family structure, something that has been largely missing in America for a long time. If the participants are careful to choose the right housemates, the results can be far more nurturing for both children and adults than the nuclear family is, or was ever capable of being.

Some group households naturally fall into patterns of child care similar to those Margaret Mead found in the "island paradise" societies she studied in Polynesia, where people other than the parents often assumed child rearing responsibilities.

Group housekeeping offers many advantages for single adults. Some would like to own homes but know that it is almost impossible for any one person to buy a house these days, or even to afford the rent on a large, roomy apartment—unless they've been highly selective about their ancestors. Others find living by themselves very lonely and would prefer to share their living quarters, even though they have not found someone with whom they want to share their beds (well, not full-time anyway). There are single people who like children and would like to have them around but are not in a position to become parents, and others who aren't sure they can stand the little tykes at all but would love a chance to find out.

Elderly people are among the loneliest individuals in our society. They often end up living alone, in constant fear of burglars or of getting hurt or sick and being unable to summon help. Many have been widowed and do not want to leave a house that is filled with happy memories but is now too large or too expensive for one person to handle. For these seniors, the physical and emotional benefits of sharing their home with younger people or with small families can be enormous, whether or not the financial benefits matter to them at all.

Students often need a quiet place to live and study. For many, dormitory life is too chaotic and distracting. For others, the cost of dormitory living is too high. Many of these students are delighted to exchange household chores, baby-sitting, yard work, and other services for someone's spare room. Not only do they make excellent

4

housemates, but they often become surrogate "big sisters" and "big brothers" in the families they live with. They get a chance to learn something about how other people live and sometimes even take a hand in child-raising, while freeing the parents to devote more of their time to their jobs and to spend some high-quality time with their children.

Other students band together to rent living space near their schools. Having lived in collective households as students, we can vouch for the fact that, through good times and bad, they produced some of the most exciting and rewarding experiences of our lives (not to mention some of the most exotic!).

And, let's not forget the fun factor. It's nice to have someone besides the cat to come home to, and it's a lot more fun to share cooking and dishwashing with another person. Housemates can be fabulous channels for other new people to come into your life. They can show you new attitudes and give you the benefit of their talents for carpentry, sewing, gardening, or whatever. No matter what your reasons for trying it, group housekeeping can certainly enrich your life.

Of course, although shared housing can solve some problems, it can also create others, particularly those that arise when a number of different personalities try to occupy the same space at the same time. Under these circumstances, no matter how well-intentioned everyone is, conflicts will arise. Yet, the blessings are usually far greater—provided you know how to minimize the problems and maximize the rewards. Even though we recognize that group housekeeping may not be for everyone, we hope to prove that it can be enormously beneficial for many people who ordinarily might never consider trying it (unless someone has turned them on to this book!).

Although we've never lived together, we have lived in a number of different kinds of group housekeeping situations over the past twenty years. We've lived in large college rooming houses with open kitchens in which twenty vastly different people managed to store and prepare their individual meals (often simultaneously) without coming to blows (well, not often, anyway!). We've shared houses and apartments with other working singles. We've enjoyed the collective child care available in married-student housing and have run our own family households when both Mommy and Daddy worked and everyone else in the house was under five years old. We've also combined forces with other single parents when our marriages ended, and have taken boarders into our own homes in exchange for everything from love to money. In short, dear readers, we've been through it all! Now, we've decided to pass on to you whatever wisdom we've gained from all those years of fun, misery, happy times, misunderstandings, friendships, feuds, unexpected rewards, enlightening experiences, and all the other positive and negative dividends of group housekeeping. And we have lots of suggestions that will help you to avoid some of the problems involved and deal successfully with others.

In case you're curious, we once considered sharing Deanna's lovely home but decided that although we work very well together, our life-styles are too divergent to be compatible on an everyday basis. Such things are important to consider when looking at potential housemates, and we have devoted a whole chapter to suggestions on how to go about selecting the right people to share your space. As in our case, friendship is not always enough, and may even turn out to be a hindrance. And you'll be surprised at some of the things that really count! To make the task easier, we've also provided questions that will help you to discover not only what kind of people you should be living with, but what kind of a person *you* are as well. We've sprinkled the book with scenarios drawn from real-life situations to give you some idea of how a variety of group housekeeping arrangements were created and to show you how other people have dealt with some of the situations that arise.

We've loaded the book with information on how to structure household schedules, how to collect and spend money for household expenses, and how to deal with sharing kitchen chores and other work that most people would rather avoid. We talk a lot about children: the unique problems and joys they can bring to a houseful of adults, and the tremendous benefits they can reap from living with other people. You'll learn how to deal with personality problems, settle disputes, assert your own needs and preferences, and generally get along with people, no matter what kind of mood they're in.

We also talk about live-in lovers and the effects they can have on the other members of a group household, the legal aspects of group housekeeping, and how to split things up without a hassle when it's time for members to go their own way.

In the course of gathering data for this book, both of us have observed a number of shared living situations and interviewed the participants. We have found that most of them are generally pleased with their living arrangements but are curious about how other people in similar situations deal with their problems. We have found, too, that people who are considering a change in life-style are even more eager for information. But what has been the most revealing is that people who once would have never even considered such a thing for themselves are dying to know what's going on. They fantasize and wonder about group housekeeping, much as the people who stayed in the East wondered what it was like for those who headed West on the wagon trains.

We believe that the people currently involved in shared living experiments are very much like the pioneers of the eighteenth and nineteenth centuries. They are hardy enough and self-confident enough to take some risks in order to try to make a better life for themselves and their children when the alternatives offered by the status quo become too confining. To these people, we dedicate this book, because we believe that they are forging new paths that will inevitably make life better for all of us.

Teona Tone and Deanna Sclar
Santa Barbara, California, 1984

CHAPTER I

Their Names Have Been Changed ... and So Have Their Lives!

How the Olsons Managed to Raise the Big Balloon

After years of penny-pinching and economizing, Gerald Olson finally earned his Ph.D. in physics and moved with his wife Nancy and their young son from Missouri to California, where he had landed an excellent position with a research firm. As a graduation present, Nancy's parents surprised the young couple with $20,000 to be used as a down payment on a house—a sum that would have secured a magnificent home in the suburbs of St. Louis.

But Nancy and Gerald had some very unpleasant news awaiting them when they arrived in San Francisco. Houses in that area—and throughout the state for that matter—were infinitely more expensive that they'd ever imagined. Not only that, local lenders demanded a 30% down payment, rather than the 20% that was usual back home! For a while it seemed as though a house was out of the question—but then, the high rent they would have to pay for a house or an apartment within commuting distance of Gerald's job indicated that their precious $20,000 might end up in a landlord's pocket, with none of the appreciation on their investment, security, tax breaks, or other advantages that owning a home provided.

The picture looked very bleak, and for a while Gerry and Nancy seriously began to consider giving up their California dreams—and a very promising job—and retreating to Missouri or to some more affordable, but less stimulating, environment. As luck would have it, a house finally turned up that was not drastically out of their financial reach. The price was reasonable (at least for Northern California!), and the owners were willing to take back a second trust deed for the balance of the down payment. Of course, the deed would fall due with a huge balloon payment at the end of three years, but Gerald and Nancy assured themselves that by that time Gerry would have received enough bonuses and raises to handle it. Besides, they were experts on scrimping and saving, weren't they? Somehow, everything would work out just fine!

Six months later, they had to face the fact that they were in over their heads. Even though Gerald's salary had seemed astronomical compared to what they'd lived on while he was at school, it just didn't seem to stretch very far in their new location. Mortgage rates were high; the cost of food, clothing, and just about everything else was escalating daily and putting money aside for what they'd come to call the "Big Balloon" was out of the question. They began to look back wistfully on their relatively carefree days in married-student housing. They'd been poor, but under much less pressure. And everyone around them had been poor, too.

The truth was, now they were not only poor, but lonely. Back home, they had been surrounded by friends, fellow students, and family. Everyone had been supportive and sympathetic. There'd been people to party with, to confide in, to rely on. Here, they felt isolated in an established neighborhood where most of the adults were older, with grown or teenage children. Nobody seemed interested in socializing with the Olsons. And, to be perfectly frank, Gerald and Nancy didn't feel they had much in common with their neighbors either!

Finally, Nancy decided to get a job. She had planned to stay home and devote herself to their son, who was just about to enter kindergarten. But wandering around the house all day worrying about their finances was driving her mad—and so was the lack of companionship. At least Gerald had someone over five years old to talk with at the office, even if the place seemed to be a total wasteland as far as socializing was concerned. Not only that, they could save her salary to pay off the Big Balloon, which hung over their heads like the sword of Damocles. What a relief it would be to know that when B day arrived, the money would be there! The more she thought about it, the better her idea seemed to be. Reluctantly, Gerald agreed that she should give it a try.

At first, things seemed to work out wonderfully. Nancy found a job fairly easily (which was a miracle in itself!), and the child-care arrangements fell into place with unexpected ease. But after a couple of months, they were forced to face the fact that since Nancy had gone to work things had gotten worse, rather than better! For one thing, the cost of day-care, commuting, lunch, and a decent work wardrobe practically equaled Nancy's salary. So much for easing their financial pressures! In fact, since she'd begun to work, all the pressures on them seemed to have increased!

Even with both of them pitching in, each day seemed to be a mad race from the kitchen table to Billy's school to their respective offices and home again. By the time they'd gotten through dinner and put Billy to bed, they were both totally exhausted. And there certainly wasn't time to keep up with the housework and the yard. Even if both of them worked all weekend, every weekend, they only seemed to get further behind.

Not only that. They never seemed to have time to play with their son anymore, and they knew that he was feeling the effects of what was becoming minimum attention from two badly overworked and overwrought parents. Besides, they missed the relaxed good times they'd had with him in what were beginning to seem like "the good old days at school."

Unsurprisingly, their own relationship was beginning to drift perilously near the rocks. Both of them needed some time off, and neither of them was getting it. They no longer seemed to have much opportunity to be close, or to have fun together; and since they tended to fall into bed exhausted, they hadn't been making love very much either. For the first time in their marriage, they began to have serious fights.

One night, they sat down at the kitchen table and considered their options. They agreed that most of the pressure and responsibility was due, directly or indirectly, to the cost of trying to pay off and maintain the house. Selling it might ease the financial pressure to some extent, but the high rentals in the area would probably keep them struggling anyway. And moving to another, less expensive neighborhood would disrupt their son's life by forcing him to leave his school and his friends just when he'd finally begun to adjust to the move from Missouri. True, it was definitely preferable to divorce, and as Gerald pointed out with rueful humor, even divorce was out of the question because they could never afford to maintain two separate residences when they were having so much trouble just paying for one!

Nancy laughed. "Well, you could share an apartment with a couple of roommates," she suggested playfully. Then suddenly her eyes widened. "Gerry," she exclaimed, "that's it! That's the answer!"

"It is?" Gerald was astounded. How could divorce solve their problems?

"Yes! It turns the whole thing around so it works to our advantage!" She was really excited now. "Listen, we've already agreed that this is a high-rental area, right? Well, we've got three bedrooms and two bathrooms and a den, and we certainly don't need all that space. Let's rent out the spare rooms!"

Gerald thought it over. "But who would want to live with us?" he asked.

"Students! We're only minutes away from the university, and lots of people hate dormitory living."

Then another idea occurred to her. (She was really rolling now.) "You know, we might even be able to find someone who would be willing to take Billy to and from school and baby-sit in the afternoons and some evenings in exchange for part of the rent!"

Gerald was getting inspired now. "Maybe we could find someone who would trade part of the rent for gardening and working around the house—you know, cleaning up and fixing things."

For the first time in months, they were grinning at each other, filled with enthusiasm.

"We'd still be getting something extra to put in the Balloon Fund," Gerald added.

"And it would be fun to have people near our own age to hang out with," Nancy suggested.

Nancy and Gerry had each spent years sharing space with other students before they'd gotten married and

then had spent some of their happiest times living under
the closely knit conditions of married-student housing,
so the prospect of sharing their home with other young
people seemed delightful. They went to bed that night
filled with optimism, eager to get their wonderful new
plan under way.

By placing ads in the student and local newspapers;
posting notices at the campus student union, cafeteria,
and bookstore; and contacting the university's employment and housing offices and a local rental agency, they
were soon able to find two young men who seemed to
fill the bill quite nicely.

Joe, a student, arranged his classes so that he could
pick up Billy after school, in exchange for reduced rent.
He had younger brothers of his own and loved to play
tag football or basketball with Billy in the yard behind
the house. That seemed to get rid of Billy's excess energy, and when Gerry and Nancy came home from work,
they'd usually find him playing quietly or watching his
favorite TV show while Joe did his homework nearby.

Joe came to occupy a unique position in the Olson
household. Billy viewed him as an older brother, and
Gerry and Nancy felt as though they'd acquired a
younger brother and a good friend. They invited him to
have dinner with them so often that he soon suggested
that they allow him to contribute to the general food fund
and take his turn at fixing meals for everyone. For the
Olsons, this was a godsend. Breakfast had been a mad
rush in a house where almost everyone had to be gone
by 8 A.M., and both of them often felt too tired to make
dinner when they arrived home at the end of the day.
Soon, even Billy was clamoring for a chance to help with
the cooking.

Matt, the other member of the group household, had
just received his graduate degree in journalism and was

working at the local newspaper. He spent much less time at home because his schedule demanded that he work until 2 A.M. to help get the morning edition out. He was delighted to live in a place where everyone left early in the morning and he could sleep undisturbed.

Matt's girlfriend, Debby, also worked on the paper and she sometimes came home to spend what was left of the night with him. At first their nocturnal arrivals disturbed Nancy, who was a light sleeper, but she soon adjusted to the slight noise of their entry and began to sleep through the night again.

Although she wasn't personally against premarital relations, she found herself worrying about how Billy would react to the fact that Matt and Debby were sleeping together when they weren't married. As it turned out, he seemed to find nothing unusual about it at all. When Debby came down to the kitchen one morning, he said to her, "You're sure lucky to get to spend the night with Matt. My mom only lets me sleep over at friends on weekends." And that was that.

Of course, problems arose that did need ironing out. In spite of his sunny disposition, Joe was a bit of a slob. Nancy didn't want him to set a bad example for Billy, and soon she found herself scolding him like a mother. But after a while, Joe got the point and not only became more conscientious about picking up after himself, he even encouraged the little boy to do the same. In a short while, Nancy found herself spending much less time on housework. And her tolerance for messes grew as she realized that Joe and Billy would pick up after themselves when the day was over. To her delight, she was soon free to spend more time playing with her son and having fun with him instead of always having to be a nagging mother and a cleaning lady.

The parking problem required another creative solution. Since every parking space within blocks of the house was filled when Matt arrived home in the middle of the night, he often parked his battered little sports car behind Gerald's car in the driveway. On those occasions, it was almost impossible to haul him, grumbling, out of bed when Gerald had to leave for work at 8 A.M. Finally, Nancy hung a pegboard in the kitchen and had everyone keep a spare set of keys there. That way, one of them could back Matt's car out of the driveway in the morning so the others could get their cars on the road.

Although Gerald wasn't able to make maintenance and gardening part of the rent deal with either of the two men, they often helped him with his chores when they were all free and puttering around the house on the weekends. And even if Matt just stood there puffing on his pipe and making conversation, Gerald found that the weeds seemed to slide out of the ground more easily.

One wonderful benefit of their new group household was that Gerald and Nancy were able to go off for occasional weekends alone together, leaving Joe to look after Billy. He soon came to look forward to these weekends almost as much as his parents did (probably because Joe was a bit of a pushover when it came to extra treats, fishing expeditions, and trips to the amusement park).

All in all, with more free time, extra income, and the chance to be alone together, group housekeeping improved the Olson's marriage immensely. It not only gave them a way to lift their financial burdens, it also improved the quality of their lives!

With a Little Courage, a Major Loss Can Be Turned into a Big Win

Mary Casper had always lived by the rules. She had graduated with honors from a small liberal arts college (which, in her milieu, meant a degree in home economics and an "MRS.") and had married John a week after graduation. John was a bright young man with good business potential, and everyone agreed that Mary had done quite well by herself in choosing to make her career as his wife. She devoted herself to becoming the perfect wife and mother and by their sixth anniversary was happily ensconced in a "picture-book" house in the suburbs, with two healthy, happy children and a successful husband. Mary felt that she had everything anyone could want, and she had every reason to believe that it would last forever.

When John informed Mary that he was getting a divorce in order to marry his secretary, the world came crashing down around her. She had focussed all of her energies on being his wife, and now she not only would not have a husband, but she also had no marketable skills with which to earn a living. In fact, she had to admit to herself that outside of being John's wife, and the children's mother, she wasn't sure if she had any identity at all!

For the first few weeks after John's announcement, Mary lived in a state of shock. When she finally began to pull out of it, she felt that it was vastly important that she keep as much of her world intact as possible. She found a lawyer and wound up with a fair divorce settlement: ample child-support payments and the right to live in the family home until the youngest child turned eighteen. "Now," she thought, "all I have to do is get myself together and my life in order." She still felt terribly bitter and hurt, but she wanted to make the transition as easy as possible for her children.

Although John's contributions covered food, clothing, and shelter, Mary soon found that the kids' music lessons, day camps, outings, and the other extras they were used to were now unaffordable. Although John loved his children, it was obviously impossible for him to pay for all of these things and handle the financial responsibilities of his new marriage as well.

"You can't get blood from a stone," Mary reminded herself and resolved to find a job to supplement his payments.

But when she began to look for work, she found that with no previous experience or office skills, she could earn very little. As in Nancy's case, practically everything she earned was swiftly consumed by after-school day-care, lunches, and carfare. Her children were already unsettled by the sudden departure of their father, and now their mother was no longer waiting for them after school. Instead, they were forced to adjust to having strangers look after them. Even in the evenings, Mary was too exhausted to give them the kind of loving attention they so badly needed. On most days, she felt too tired even to cook dinner for them, let alone play with them before bedtime! After devoting her life to being their mother, she now found herself caught in a tragic paradox: Her attempts to provide a full life for her children were instead depriving them of the most essential experience of all—a loving and attentive mother. Mary felt guilty, depressed, inadequate, and angry at the world.

Because she was basically a positive and resourceful woman, Mary was determined to raise her kids in the best way possible. When she saw that her resentment and depression were affecting them more negatively than anything else, she immediately arranged to see a counselor at a local family clinic. During their first few meetings, she was able to vent a good deal of her anger and frustration. To her amazement, that seemed to give her some relief and helped to improve her spirits. But she still faced what seemed like insurmountable problems.

When the counselor suggested that she join a single-parents' support group, Mary responded, "I'm not interested in meeting any men, especially divorced ones. I'm still too hurt about what happened with John." The counselor agreed that she was wise in not wanting to jump into another relationship so soon, but explained that the group would put Mary in contact with other people who were dealing with some of the same problems she was facing.

Mary was still skeptical. "If we can't handle our own problems, how can we help each other?" she demanded.

"It helps to share," replied the counselor, "and human beings are very innovative. You might find some unexpected alternatives that would be very helpful to you. At any rate, at least you'd no longer feel that you were the only one in the world who'd had the rug pulled out from under you. Why don't you give it a try?"

Mary finally agreed to attend a few sessions on a trial basis. After all, she really had nothing to lose, and if there was a remote chance she might gain something, why not?

The group presented some shocking revelations to a woman with Mary's conservative background. On the very first evening, she learned that several of the members were involved in group living situations. She had always assumed that such arrangements were slightly illicit. Visions of free sex and drug use in hippie-style communes came to her mind. Or welfare families stuffed into crowded slum apartments. But to her amazement, the people she encountered who were sharing living space were neither poor, nor criminal, nor long-haired bohemians. They were regular, middle-class citizens. Ordinary people, just like herself! She found them to be well-dressed, well-educated, respectable people. And they were solving the same problems she was trying to deal with in isolation by sharing their homes with other adults, or with another single-parent family. When the meeting was over, she went home with her head spinning to digest what she'd heard.

After thinking things over for a few days, Mary timidly began to consider taking similar steps to solve her problems. Her house had a garage that had been converted into a large recreation room with its own bathroom and entrance. It could easily serve as a studio apartment. . . .

The following week she went back to the group armed with a list of questions. To her delight, Ellie Summerson, who lived in a group household, invited her to visit her home and check things out for herself. "Why don't you come to dinner on Thursday and see for yourself that none of us has two heads or any other abnormalities as a result of sharing a house," she said, laughing. "I'll answer all the questions you can think of. I think I know them all by now, I've been doing this for five years!"

"Then why do you still come to this support group?" asked Mary.

"Because being a single parent isn't easy, no matter how you cut it. With the support group as an outlet for my gripes and tears, I find I don't overburden the people I live with and we have a better relationship. Besides, I like the people."

Mary could see that the other members of the group were very fond of the cheerful and outgoing Ellie, too.

She was obviously a "people person," especially compared to Mary, who was fairly shy and had a tendency to keep to herself. Mary wondered if her reticent nature would be an obstacle to sharing her home with other people. Her house had always been a refuge for her, and the thought of sharing it seemed like an invasion of her privacy.

Visiting Ellie's house failed to convince Mary that group housekeeping was the right thing for her. It was a boisterous, messy place. True, it was relaxed and cheerful, but to Mary it seemed noisy and full of confusion. It seemed to overflow with Ellie's two high-spirited teenagers and her housemate's active toddlers.

"I just love little kids," bubbled Ellie, "and this way I don't have to bother giving birth to any more myself!"

But Mary knew that she couldn't handle this kind of scene on a day-to-day basis. She needed a peaceful place to come home to. And she was afraid that her quiet, well-behaved children might learn bad habits from living with someone else's offspring. Besides, she might clash with the other parent over rules and discipline. And what about childhood diseases?

Mary was on her way home, feeling dejected and hopeless, when a new thought suddenly hit her. She could simply rent space to a single adult! She conjured up a picture of a quiet, single, working woman who would be gone most of the time, leaving her alone in her house to spend the day in privacy. Then she realized that even with the extra rent money, she'd probably still have to work, at least part-time, to supplement her income. So Mary decided to try to find a nice grandmotherly person who would bounce the children on her knee and have delicious dinners waiting when Mary came home from work.

This cozy mental picture lifted Mary's spirits considerably. Her gloom was shot through with rays of hope. However, in the days that followed, she found herself curiously blocked when it came to taking the first steps toward finding the right person to live with. For a while, she tried to set the idea aside, but it kept returning to her, especially when she was feeling tired and frustrated. It would be so nice to be able to cut back the hours she spent at work and to have some time to be with the kids!

Finally, she brought up her problem at one of the support group meetings. She knew she was reluctant to run an ad in a newspaper. No matter what anyone said, it just felt kind of tacky—not to mention risky. Even if she decided to rent a room and bath to a single woman, how should she go about finding the right person?

This time it wasn't Ellie who supplied the answer, it was a new member of the group named Georgia.

"I recently had the same problem," Georgia said in a soft, almost timid voice. "I was afraid to advertise, too. I didn't think I could handle having a bunch of strangers come to my home and know where I lived and that I was alone. And I didn't have any idea of how to interview them, or tell if they were safe to live with. Then, someone told me about the roommate referral service here in town. It's quite well-established, in fact they place a lot of students for the university. I checked them out, and they informed me that no one they'd ever placed had ever run off with the silver or murdered the lady of the house," she added, laughing a little at herself. "The worst thing that ever happened was that the people's personalities just didn't 'click' and the agreement was dissolved. In fact, they assured me that they'd learned a great deal about matching people over the years, and that their success rate was really excellent."

Georgia told Mary that the referral service had screened all the applicants' references, individual needs, and life-styles thoroughly before introducing them to her. Although few services are usually willing to go this far, they had even arranged for her to meet the prospective applicants at their office when she told them how frightened she was of having strangers come directly to her home. Then, if she felt comfortable with someone, she had the option of arranging for them to visit the house.

On the strength of Georgia's recommendation, Mary visited the referral service and paid them $35 to set the search in motion. But when the first few people she interviewed seemed entirely unsuitable, she was about to give up completely. Then she got a call one afternoon at work.

"I've got a lady here I think you should meet," said the woman from the service. "I think you two would get along very well. Our offices will be closed this evening, so would you be willing to see her at your home?"

"I guess so," said Mary wearily. She really had lots of chores to deal with, but something in the woman's voice told her to say yes.

After dinner, Mary asked the children to wash the dishes while she straightened up the house, regretting that she'd set up the interview. The ironing would have to wait and so would the curtains she was sewing for the kitchen. All she really wanted to do was to take a hot bath and go to bed. Instead, she would have to talk with a complete stranger about living in her home. It was almost too much to handle.

Mary began to think about how her life used to be, when John was still there to care for her and support her. By the time the doorbell rang, she was practically in tears. She pulled herself together and answered the door.

Mary found herself looking into the eyes of a slim woman of about her age who was holding a pretty little girl by the hand. For a moment, Mary lost her self-control and blurted out, "But I told the lady at the service that I only wanted a single lady without children!"

"Yes," the woman replied, in a warm, mellow voice with a trace of a middle-European accent, "she told me that and she even suggested that I leave Melissa behind when I first came to see you. But that didn't seem honest, so if you do not care to talk to me, I understand,"

The woman turned to go, but Mary stopped her. For some reason, she felt a rush of warmth toward this dignified woman and wanted to be her friend. Perhaps it was because the woman seemed to project an air of quiet calmness and assurance that Mary needed so desperately and couldn't seem to find in herself.

"No, please don't go," she found herself saying. "Since you came all the way out here, I'd like you to at least stay for a cup of tea."

As they talked together at the kitchen table, Mary learned that the woman, Hilda Brandt, was the daughter of immigrant parents who had raised her to be a concert pianist. Instead, she had married a violinist and had given up her career to become a wife and mother. Her husband had died of leukemia a year ago and had only left behind enough insurance money to pay for his funeral. Hilda had been giving piano lessons to support herself and her daughter. Since she went to her students' homes to teach, she had baby-sitting problems, too. And now she had another, even worse problem.

"We have always lived in the same apartment," she explained, "and the landlord has been very good about not raising the rent. But now the building has been sold and the rents have doubled. There is no way I can afford that much money, and every other apartment I've looked at costs at least as much. I have to leave by the end of the month, which is next week, and I was getting desperate until someone suggested the referral service that sent me here."

Mary looked with compassion at Hilda. She knew from her own experience how helpless and frightening it was to be alone. How much worse it must be to face having no roof over your head, especially when you have a child to care for! She looked at Melissa, who was playing with her children at the far end of the room. The kids were getting along famously, and she found she not only liked this solemn, gray-eyed woman, but she liked her little girl as well. She showed Hilda the studio apartment and agreed to let her move in on a trial basis, although she suggested that Hilda keep trying to find another place, just in case things didn't work out.

Mary needn't have worried. Her new expanded family worked out beautifully. Because she and Hilda had similar natures and basic values about child rearing, housekeeping, and cooking, things ran more smoothly in the household than either of them had dared to dream they could. The children got along better than most real siblings, because Mary's children were thrilled to have a new "sister," and Melissa was delighted to no longer be an only child.

Hilda's busy time for teaching was after school and in the early evenings, so she spent most mornings at home. Mary, in turn, arranged to take a part-time job so she could be with the children when they came home from school. Even before the two agreed to share the cooking, Hilda began to bake goodies for everyone, and Mary and the children would come home to find the house filled with warmth and the delicious aroma of the surprise snacks that often awaited them.

When they decided to keep a common larder, Hilda usually made breakfast and did the shopping in the morning, while Mary prepared dinner for them all, if Hilda had not surprised them with something special. Because they shared the housekeeping in the kitchen and the living room, Mary found that cleaning the rest of the house was easy. And both families pitched in on the yard work and other maintenance. Mary cared for Melissa after school, and Hilda gave the boys piano lessons in return.

Mary's life became much more calm and happy. To her surprise, she found that she really enjoyed the daily presence of another adult in her life. Neither she nor Hilda felt ready to look for a new mate; they each had their own grief to deal with first, but they still needed the support of another adult, and they found that support in each other. Even when their schedules were busy, they often found the time to sit and have a cup of tea together late at night, when they could relax and talk about their lives, their children, and the events of the day.

Their arrangement has lasted for several years. Before either of them was ready to date, it gave them the companionship they needed. When they began dating again, they were able to support one another by babysitting and by being there to talk over the feelings that inevitably arose. Today, Mary is about to remarry and Hilda is dating an electronics engineer who plays the organ for her church on Sundays. Their group housekeeping arrangement will probably not last much longer, but it has provided a vital element in their lives, and the two of them will probably always remain close friends. What was originally a "picture-book" home for a model nuclear family has turned out to be a creative environment for two gallant women and their children.

THE YOUNG PIONEERS

The Millers and the Jasons found themselves faced with a completely different situation. Both were professional couples who had delayed buying houses and rearing children until they had all established themselves in their chosen careers.

Unfortunately, when each couple finally decided to start thinking about buying a home, the housing market was so inflated that anything suitable was quite beyond their means. Rents were going up as well, and it seemed foolish to throw money away on rent when houses afforded such tax advantages. Their growing desire to start families made the situation even worse because it meant that not only would each family need more space, but the earning power of the wives would be cut back while they tended to nursing chores during the first year of motherhood. And then, of course, the couples would have to come up with still more money for child care when the women returned to work. Becky Miller kept saying she was afraid her biological time clock would run out before her family ever got started!

The two couples had been friends for some time, and while they were discussing their mutual problems over dinner one evening, Ralph Miller laughingly commented that perhaps if they put their money together they might have enough for the down payment on just one house.

"Yeah," Sarah Jason had added sarcastically, "and then we could take turns living in it every other week!"

"Or, we could flip a coin to see who would get to keep the place," suggested Fred Jason, "winner take all."

"Hey, wait a minute!" Becky was suddenly serious. "Why couldn't we all live in it together? After all, we get along pretty well, and we'd be able to get a really large house—big enough to have room for a couple of babies."

"We could share a baby-sitter and raise the babies together!" Sarah added enthusiastically. She had a dreamy look in her eyes.

"Now, hold on there!" exclaimed Ralph. "Just because I make a crazy suggestion, you two don't have to take it seriously, let alone make it even crazier!"

"But it's not crazy at all," Becky promptly responded. "If we did it right, I think it might work."

"You know, it might be worth looking into," mused Sarah. "It's not any crazier than some of the things we've fantasized about, like moving to the South Pacific. And as Becky always says, 'I want to have my baby before the year 2000!'"

By the end of the evening, the two couples had agreed to look into what it would take to buy a house together. After some research, they decided that it just might work out. All four started making lists of what they thought they wanted, and the comparisons were often hilarious.

"Well, what we need here is a large Victorian house with a Spanish-style central patio, both convenient to the city and well out in the quiet suburbs," Fred said, after going over their lists. "It should have at least four bedrooms ("plus a maid's room," added Becky, looking over his shoulder) and at least two studies, a family room, a rec room for the kids, a huge kitchen, a sauna, a hot tub, and a tree with a tire-swing in the garden."

"Don't forget the laundry room, the workshop, the four-car garage, and the guest rooms," added Ralph.

"And the large attic for rainy days," Sarah reminded them.

"It looks as though we might be better off buying a small town," said Fred wryly. "Look guys, I think we'd better be prepared to cut back on our expectations!"

As strange as it may seem, they actually did manage to finally find a house that suited everyone (with a lot of compromising here and there) and the bargaining began. The final transaction was so complicated that it nearly convinced one real estate agent to leave the profession and almost drove the couples' lawyers crazy. But at last the place was out of escrow and the Millers and the Jasons became the proud owners of a large old Victorian house (Becky won that one) close to the downtown area where they all worked. The house was located on a quiet, tree-lined street in a slightly seedy neighborhood that was in the process of being restored to the charm it had once displayed at the turn of the century. It suited their social consciousness perfectly and promised to provide enough living space for both families. They treated the house as a business venture in which each of them was an investor with a piece of the action, and they settled down to fix it up themselves.

The first floor, which contained a large kitchen, a dining room, and a living room, seemed ideally designed for feeding both families and entertaining guests.

By the toss of a coin, the Jasons won the second floor, which had three rooms and a bath. The Millers got to occupy the three rooms and bath on the top floor (just under the wonderful attic where the kids could play on rainy days). Ralph planned to turn one of those rooms into a study where he and Becky could work after office hours or just relax if they wanted to spend a quiet family evening at home.

Unfortunately, their divergence of tastes and different priorities created a lot of problems when it came to decorating the house. Every minor decision seemed to turn into a major debate. The choice of wallpaper for the dining room called for endless summit meetings, and there was a heated controversy between the two women over gas versus electricity when it came to buying a new stove for the kitchen.

The living room was even worse, with both couples evenly divided on whether the woodwork should be repainted or stripped and stained. Fred Jason and Becky Miller stoutly maintained that painting would be quicker and cheaper, while their spouses thought it was totally immoral to perpetuate the desecration that had been wrought on that beautiful oak.

Work soon crawled to a stop, and for a while it seemed as though everything was going to fall apart even before they moved in. If things were this much of a problem already, what would it be like when they were all trying to live together?

Then help arrived in the form of a friend of Sarah's who was a retired interior decorator. After years of dealing with similar problems, she had become a woman of infinite tact and discretion. She took a motherly interest in the two couples and was intrigued by the unique possibilities that the project offered. She told them, "Some of my happiest memories date from the time when my husband and I shared a house with another young couple during the Second World War. Our first child had just been born and I knew nothing about babies. I was so glad to have another woman around to give me advice. That experience convinced me that the so-called nuclear family was not the only possible arrangement and maybe not even the best!" When the war ended, she had never had the chance to repeat the experiment, and now she dearly wanted to help the Millers and the Jasons to pioneer a new way of life.

So Mildred Fletcher offered her assistance in renovating the house. She arrived one morning and simply took over, but with such tact and grace that nobody objected. She came up with solutions that met with everyone's approval. ("Why not buy one of each?" she suggested to settle the Great Kitchen Debate. "Feeding two families simultaneously will probably require more than four burners anyway!") In addition to providing helpful suggestions, she got right in and worked with them, up to her elbows in dirt and sawdust. It was Mildred who was always there to oversee the plumbers, electricians, and painters when everyone else was at work, and in less than six months, the house was ready.

During that time, by working together so intensely, the couples had adjusted to each other's individual preferences and ways of doing things. Consequently, the actual transition to group housekeeping was not as traumatic as it might have been.

The Millers' baby was born about four months before the Jasons'. Although Ralph took as much time off from work as he could to be with Becky and his daughter during those first crucial months, Sarah spent a lot of time with them as well. She had never been around an infant and the experience was invaluable to her. When her son was born, the whole group began to work together like a real family. During the first two years, both women were able to return to work on a half-time basis by babysitting for each other. Eventually, they hired a housekeeper to watch both babies and do the cooking and cleaning, so they were able to resume their careers fulltime, knowing that their children were getting the best of care and that they had each other for company until their parents returned home each evening.

It is interesting to note that another two families in our area have recently solved similar problems by buying one large piece of land in the country and building two entirely separate homes, joined together by a service area. In this way, they managed to avoid the red tape and expense involved in a land-split, and getting the Zoning Department's approval of two sets of plans and site modifications. Because they have been able to buy building materials together, they have been able to obtain everything they require at the discounted prices available on large orders. They even bought and removed enough old Spanish roof tiles from a mansion that was being renovated to roof both homes spectacularly!

What is there to learn from all of these stories? First, that living with other people can solve a whole spectrum of problems, from loneliness and the need for mutual support and companionship to creating new ways to find affordable housing. It can free parents to pursue their careers, provide valuable experiences for children, and create environments where students can live cheaply and learn things from both the older and younger members of their new "families" that may prove to be more valuable than what they learn at school.

Second, that the key is to become very clear about what it is you need and to be as precise as possible about the qualities and characteristics that you require in a prospective housemate. And to trust that once you really know what you want, you will be able to create a reality in which you will find it.

The third thing is to be willing to be open and flexible about adapting to the opportunities that present themselves. Mary Casper was sure that what she needed was a nice grandmotherly person. What she eventually received was the chance to live with another young mother who also became a cherished friend.

The variations are endless, the opportunities limitless. If you are willing to take the risks and to trust a stranger, you may find that the rewards of group housekeeping go far beyond your fondest hopes and dreams!

Now let's explore some practical techniques that will help you to draw an accurate profile of the kind of people you will find compatible as housemates. Then we'll suggest where and how to find them. It may not come as a surprise that you must first evaluate what *you* are like to live with, so we'll provide a way for you to do some personal stocktaking with this in mind. We'll also talk about that first important interview, and when you should be willing to let go of your expectations and rely on your intuition. So let's stop talking about other people for a while and get down to the basics!

CHAPTER II

"Somebody Out There Likes Me!": How to Find the Right People to Live With

Even if you've already decided to rent out that spare room, how do you go about finding a housemate who *won't* turn out to be the Boston Strangler and who *will* turn out to be pleasant company? How do you advertise without bringing a host of unsuitable or unsavory applicants into your home? And how do you screen applicants to be sure you are getting someone who is not only compatible but trustworthy? What kind of references do you ask for and how do you check them out? Do you need to interview everyone who responds, or are there some shortcuts you can take to weed out the unsuitable ones before they get to your house? What kind of questions can you ask without giving offense? And what kind of questions should you be willing to answer?

Sharing your living space with other human beings is a highly personal experience, and if you treat it as such from the very beginning, you will have greater success in finding compatible housemates. Surprisingly, few people take the trouble to get very clear about what type of housemate would fit most easily into their life-style. Whether they are choosing future mates or housemates, the leave the matter pretty much to chance—often with disastrous consequences in both cases.

VISUALIZE YOUR PERFECT HOUSEMATE

Before you actually start to look for a housemate, we recommend that you take the time to sit down with a pencil and paper and write a description of the most perfect housemate you can envision. Don't stop to criticize or correct apparent contradictions, just write down whatever comes into your head. You can always analyze it later. Include as many details as you can, no matter how irrelevant they may seem to you. The list is endless and the best way to go about it is to get into "free-fall" and just follow your imagination wherever it leads.

Be honest. If you weigh two hundred pounds and would be uncomfortable living with a sylphlike individual, acknowledge it. If you're a back-to-the-Bible Christian, you probably wouldn't be happy living with a confirmed atheist. How do you feel about living with someone of another race? You need to decide what the real limits of your tolerance are, regardless of what you feel they *should* be.

Little things can lead to major conflicts if you don't anticipate them! Coming up with a clear picture of your perfect housemate will call for some serious soul-searching and thought on your part, so take the time to go over your profile carefully after you've created it spontaneously. Even though you aren't likely to find someone who meets all of your preferences, you will have a much better idea of just who it is you are looking for, and this will definitely increase your chances of finding someone compatible.

As an added bonus, a clear picture of the sort of person you are seeking may also give you valuable clues as to where to look for the most likely candidates. For instance, if you are seriously into sailing and would like a housemate who shares your enthusiasm for boats, you might want to advertise in a local sailing association newsletter or to post a notice on the bulletin board at a nearby yacht club or marina. If much of your life centers around your church, make sure your minister knows you have a room available and put notices on the church bulletin board and in the newsletter, too.

Following are some areas to consider while you compose your list of preferred characteristics:

Money or Services?

If you are looking for someone to share your living quarters, rather than attempting to rent space in someone else's establishment, consider your priorities as well as your motives for sharing your home. For some of us, the financial benefits come first. Others would be happy to receive less rent if they could find someone who was extra-good company or who would be available for babysitting. Do you simply want someone who will pay you so much per month in rent, or would you prefer someone who would participate in the upkeep of the house and the yard, or take it over completely, in exchange for paying less rent or no rent at all? What are these services worth to you?

If you plan to trade part of the rent for a service, we've found that it is wiser to keep a record of the hours your tenant has worked and deduct an agreed upon sum per hour from his or her rent, at the end of the month. Just how you record this, and whether or not you exchange actual money, will depend, among other things, on your tax situation. Somehow, arrangements where the tenant is told, "I should charge you $400, but if you will take care of the place for me I will make it $200," just don't work out. Many tenants tend to forget that they have been given a lower rental and come to see their contributions of labor as either more significant than they really are or as acts of generosity on their part. If they get pressured, they tend to do less and less, without paying more and more.

If you really need the money to keep up with your own financial obligations, beware of renting to relatives or close friends. It is much harder to dun people you love if they get into financial straits and are unable to pay the rent on time. They may also be tempted to use the rent to pay creditors who are more likely to make trouble if they aren't paid on time. Whoever you rent to, be sure that they have excellent financial references.

The Numbers Game

How many housemates are you looking for? In most cases, the number of individuals you can successfully include in a group household depends on how many rooms you have to spare and how many bathrooms are available. Renting one room to two people who do not know each other can create problems. Renting a room and bath to a married couple may work out very well in some cases. So ask yourself if you would be willing to rent the spare bedroom to a couple.

To keep things simple, let's assume for the moment that you are only looking for one housemate. If you are really looking for more than one person, simply note which characteristics must apply to everyone and where only one individual with a single attribute would suffice.

For example: You might be satisfied with one roommate who is capable of doing the heavy yard work and another who would be willing to act as a surrogate grandmother to your children—but each of them would have to be a nonsmoker.

Sexual Preferences

Must your housemate be of a particular sex? If you're a woman, would you only consider living with another woman? Or are you willing to share your home with a man? These days, it would not necessarily be taken for granted that you were sleeping together, and there are many practical reasons why a single woman might welcome having a man around the house. If you are a man, the reverse applies.

On the other hand, let's be frank. Perhaps you are considering taking on a housemate of the opposite sex because you are secretly hoping that you might become romantically involved. Or are you determined to keep that part of your life separate? In other words, are you looking for a live-in lover or simply for a housemate? There's no need for moral judgments here; just be clear about what you want. If the former is true, it may take much longer to find a suitable person to share your home. It is one thing to rent out a room and another to commit your heart!

How do you feel about homosexuality? Whether you are gay or straight, do you have strong feelings about living with someone who does not share your particular inclination?

What about extramarital sex? We discuss the whole issue of live-in lovers in Chapter V, but you'll need to know, on a gut level, whether you will mind if your housemates invite dates to sleep over and whether a prospective housemate will be happy about your conducting love affairs on the premises.

How about modesty? If you're used to walking around the house undressed, or you and your friends enjoy skinny-dipping in the hot tub or pool, then you'd better find a housemate who can handle it. On the other hand, if you're a very modest person, you'll probably want to live with someone who prefers to cover up around the house.

Oscar or Felix?

What are your preferences with regard to neatness or sloppiness? Some people are extremely fastidious, and even if the door to a sloppy housemate's room is kept closed the fact that the room is messy remains a constant source of irritation. Other people would much rather live with someone who can put up with their own sloppy habits without becoming a nag or huffily doing all the work themselves. Keep "The Odd Couple" in mind on this one!

Breaking the Sound Barriers

What are your limits when it comes to noise? When you live with other people, you must live with the sounds they create. We're not just talking about loud voices, but loud radios, TVs, stereo systems, musical instruments, typewriters, sewing machines, pets, and constantly ringing phones. Whether you are sensitive to these intrusions, or are likely to be responsible for creating noise in this way, be sure to find a roommate who will be compatible.

Recreational Drugs

How about smoking? Drinking? Marijuana? If you in-
dulge in any of these, or have a strong distaste for them,
you will probably feel most comfortable with someone
who shares your attitudes. If you are a former alcoholic
or are trying to kick tobacco or pot, you certainly don't
need to bring temptation into your nest.

The Social Scene

While we're on the subject of partying, do you want a
housemate who will bring a lot of new people into your
life? Or would you prefer a quiet soul who doesn't entertain much? Even if you don't have to join the festiv-
ities, you will still have to put up with the traffic, the
noise, and the effects on the kitchen and the bathroom.
Of course, if you are shy, or new in town, a social-but-
terfly roommate can be a tremendous asset! Another
thing to think about is whether you prefer someone who
is away a good deal of the time, or are you looking for
some companionship.

Consider Children

Some potential housemates may be single parents without custody but with visitation rights. Would you be willing to have a child or children around the house on weekends or holidays? You might want to meet the kids before
making a decision. On the other hand, if you have children, do you want to share your home with someone else
who has kids, or someone who doesn't? If this is a consideration, be sure to read chapter VII closely.

What about Pets?

Would you welcome a watchdog you didn't have to feel responsible for feeding, bathing, and walking? Are you allergic to cats? How do you feel about living with birds? Or snakes? Pets have personalities, too, and must be considered as members of any household. Whether they are "yours, mine, or ours," you and any potential housemate must be in agreement. We tell you what to do if a roommate's canary devours your cat in Chapter III.

The Age Factor

You may want to rent to a student, to bring some youthful energy into your life. Or you may desire someone of your own age, or older. Although people tend to choose to live with others their own age, we've found that there are enormous benefits to be gained from living with someone who is significantly older or younger than yourself. Several such instances come up in the course of this book.

Consult the Rest of Your Family

If other members of your family live with you, it is wise to ask each of those above the age of three to conjure up their perfect housemate, too. Then, sit down together and listen to everyone's input, noting the similarities and the differences in what's important to each family member. You may find some surprises here, and it's a good opportunity to learn a lot about the other members of your household. If your three-year-old son wants a roommate who would be willing to read bedtime stories to him, he might be giving you a hint that he needs more adult attention than he is currently getting. Or your ten-year-old daughter might want someone to play baseball with—and you never even dreamed she was into sports! (Remember the touching scene in *Mary Poppins* where the children revise their father's list of qualifications for a nanny? Your children may have just as much insight into the sort of housemate your family really requires.)

Even if family members' suggestions should prove impractical, other benefits of such a conference are that they will know you are taking their input seriously and you will get a chance to express your views of what a good housemate should be like. (If you're lucky, some of your existing "housemates" will get the hint!)

What Kind of a Housemate Are *You*?

As you may have noticed, many of the questions about your preference in roommates deal with your own idiosyncrasies in order to determine the specific attributes a housemate should have in order to be compatible with you and your family (even if your "family" consists of yourself and a potted palm). In truth, the real object of asking such questions is to find the answer to the most vital question of all: What are *you* like to live with? It is very important to have an objective view of yourself when you are considering living with someone else. It can make a big difference in whom you choose, and whether the alliance works out successfully. Some people go through a host of roommates and never get in touch with the fact that they are rather difficult to live with themselves!

Hunting for the Perfect Housemate

When you are pretty clear on the type of housemate you are seeking and have recovered from the shock of getting in touch with what you are probably like to live with, just how do you go about finding the paragon of perfection who is most likely to fill the bill?

Look in Your Own Backyard

As we've said before, your own interests and priorities can often provide clues to good sources of potential roommates. Often an organization or church you belong to can put you in touch with compatible potential housemates. Check these sources to find out if they have a newsletter or other means of posting a notice at little or no cost.

Emma Moss, a widow in her late fifties, decided to rent out one of the rooms in her large apartment rather than move to a smaller place. Because she lived near a university and had always liked young people, at first she thought of renting to a student. But for some reason, the very thought of placing an ad in the local paper or registering with the university's housing bureau made her terribly uneasy.

At our suggestion, she went through the process outlined above. She also asked other people who knew her well what she was like to live with. Above all, she was honest with herself about her priorities and attitudes.

When all the data was in, Emma realized that she would be much more comfortable with a woman her own age, who shared her interests and would even be free to travel with her at times. She wanted a pleasant companion, rather than the lively stimulation a college student was likely to provide.

This information also indicated that there was probably no need for Emma to advertise in the newspaper, or to contact a roommate referral service to find the person she wanted. She belonged to several social groups with many members her own age, and so she simply put a notice in their newsletters, detailing the type of person she wanted.

> MATURE WIDOW seeks housemate who shares her interest in orchids, classical music, or travel. Sunny spacious room and bath in large apartment near the university offers right blend of privacy and companionship. $350/mo. Available June 1.

Within a short time, she had several applicants and was able to choose a housemate that suited her perfectly. And as an extra bonus, she eventually became friends with a few of the others who had contacted her because they had similar interests.

Gary Hill, a young electronics technician, found a suitable roommate at work. He had just finished his stint in the navy and had landed a good job with a large electronics firm in Santa Barbara. He arrived in town knowing no one and without a place to live. Luckily, his Aunt Louise knew Teona's mother and had heard that we were writing this book right in his new hometown. When he called, we gave him a quickie version of this chapter over the phone.

Gary felt that because of his years in the navy, he'd be happiest living in a group household with several other young men, preferably ones involved in electronics in some way. He was not ready for a family atmosphere yet and thought he'd like to have roommates he could go out and party with when his working hours were over.

Because Gary's time and finances were limited, we suggested that he ask around at work and post a notice on the bulletin board. We also advised him to register at a local roommate referral service that screened applicants and matched them according to personality traits, financial situation, and mutual interests.

It didn't take Gary long to find exactly what he wanted. There are a lot of single electronics engineers in Santa Barbara, and many of them own homes and rent out the spare bedrooms. Soon Gary had joined two other men he'd met at work in a house that was close to his office. He is very happy with this arrangement because it not only costs him less than it would if he lived alone, but he now has companionship in the evenings. His roommates have introduced him to several women, and his social life is already active.

Free Advertising

There's a wide variety of free resources available to help you to find the right housemate. Use your imagination! Some examples follow:

Bulletin Boards

Your place of employment may also have a bulletin board where you could put up a notice. Many neighborhood grocery stores and laundromats have bulletin boards for the use of their patrons, but you might not want to have to deal with the unscreened applicants who might be attracted. The bulletin board at your child's school may be useful if you are looking for another single-parent family to live with. At any rate, when using any public board, give no more than your first name and phone number. Later in this chapter we'll get into ways to screen applicants over the phone that should help you to eliminate any weirdos before they get to your doorstep.

Networking

Put the word out among your friends and business associates—this is called "networking" and is one of the most effective ways of finding out about anything. It is particularly effective for finding housemates because your friends will probably have other acquaintances and associates with similar interests. Or at least close enough for comfort. You could also ask your hairdresser or barber. They usually have a pretty good idea of their customers' personalities and circumstances and often hear if someone is looking for a new housemate.

Local Educational Institutions

If you are willing to rent to a student, try a nearby college, university, or technical school. They usually have an office where you can list your available space for free. Remember, all students are not wet-behind-the-ears undergraduates; many are graduate students or adult returnees who would make quiet, responsible housemates. And sometimes instructors, professors, and other staff members are in need of housing near the school and would welcome the chance to live in a group household—after all, schools do not pay very well and their employees often need to cut corners wherever they can.

Newspapers

Most newspapers have "Rooms for Rent" and "Personals" columns in the classified section. Remember—the same caution about unscreened applicants that we mentioned in connection with bulletin boards also applies here. Some newspapers also offer you the option of using a box number instead of a phone number. Although replies by mail slow the process a little, they do increase your privacy. And although you may not be a handwriting analyst, very often correspondence can provide very good clues to what a person is like.

In addition to the major papers, we suggest that you find out what little neighborhood weekly publications might exist. This is most handy if you are looking for a room or house to share in a specific area of town, near your children's schools or your place of work. (Teona once found a pasture for her two horses first, and then looked for a house nearby.)

Like Emma Moss, be sure to indicate the four W's in your ad:

Who you are (not by name, but in general terms) and whom you'd like to live with
What your space is like and what it will cost (or what kind of space you'd like to rent)
Where your space is—the locality, *not* your address (or where you'd like to live)
When you, or your space, will be available

If you are offering a special proposition such as space or a rent reduction in exchange for services, be sure to mention this.

Rental Agencies and Referral Services

Finally, there are the rental agencies and roommate referral services. These vary quite widely in their fees, the services they offer, and in efficiency. For a fee of $35 to $50, many rental agencies will provide computerized lists, organized according to price, and will update those lists for three to six months. These lists are usually intended for people who are looking for apartments or houses, not housemates. Some rental agencies do have specific lists of "Shared Rentals" or "Rooms for Rent," but they are not geared for matching personalities, interests, etc. That is left entirely up to you.

It has been our experience that roommate referral services try to do at least some screening of applicants. They will probably ask you to fill out a questionnaire similar to the one we have included in this chapter. The fees they charge are comparable to rental agencies', but their services are much closer to those you probably want, whether you intend to list a room for rent or are trying to find one. If you have space to share, listing it with a referral service has several advantages. Some only charge the party who is looking for a place to share and offer their services free to people with places to rent, in order to obtain as many listings as possible. The money you save by not having to pay for newspaper ads can be enough to go out and celebrate with the great new housemate they found you (after screening out all the losers beforehand!).

There is another source you might want to consider when looking for people to live with. The National Shared Housing Resource Center is a national center for more than 300 local and regional shared housing agencies across the country. They specialize in helping people to find compatible living situations, with special emphasis on single parents, the elderly, and handicapped people. They also publish the *Shared Housing Quarterly*, a bulletin that lists all the self-help books available. If you contact them, they will be able to provide you with the phone number and address of an agency in your area. In our city, an agency called Share-A-Home not only brings prospective housemates together but also sponsors workshops and problem-solving sessions.

Here's how to get in touch with the national center:

National Shared Housing and Resource Center
6344 Greene Street
Philadelphia, PA 19144
Telephone: (215) 848-1220

THE SELECTION PROCESS

There are three major phases in the process of selecting a roommate: preliminary screening over the phone, a face-to-face interview, and the careful checking of personal and financial references.

The Telephone Interview: "You Don't Know Me, But . . ."

So you've decided what type of a housemate you want, you've advertised, and one evening the phone rings and a voice on the other end says, "You don't know me, but I'm calling about the room you have for rent." Or perhaps you're the one doing the calling. In either case, how do you get to know each other? How personal can you get? And what information do you have the right to keep to yourself?

The first phone call is very important. For one thing, it can put an end to the necessity for having to endure an interview at all, because you may find out right then and there that you just aren't meant for one another. You can tell a lot about people from just talking to them over the phone. Focus on picking up every available clue, such as tone of voice, willingness to listen to what you have to say, which questions they are quite willing to answer and which cause them to hesitate or embarrass them, and the things they want to know about you.

Even background noises may be clues to a person's compatibility: If you're looking for a housemate who loves peace and quiet, and the person on the other end of the line is yelling over a combination of loud rock music, children screaming, and pots and pans clattering, you can probably safely end the conversation right there.

Go with your hunches. Often we perceive things on a subconscious level that we cannot rationalize but that usually turn out to be incredibly accurate. If, for any reason, you decide that you are not interested in interviewing certain applicants, be very clear with them. It's fine to tell them what you are looking for, but even if they stoutly maintain that they fit every category, go with your feelings if you do not feel right about them. Simply tell them that you are not interested and thank them for calling. By not having them know where you live, you do not run the risk that they will show up on your doorstep to continue the conversation.

Use the first phone call to get some basic information. We've provided two checklists—one for people who have space to rent, and one for those who are looking for a place to live—to help you to cover the most important points. Keep it friendly and casual, be sure to talk about your own requirements, and chat a little just to get a sense of what the person on the other end of the line is like. Take notes, and avoid becoming confused after several phone interviews by jotting down your impressions on the same page—for example, "The woman with the Saint Bernard" or "The man with the charming Southern accent"—to help you to identify each individual.

PHONE INTERVIEW CHECKLIST
FOR THOSE WITH SPACE TO RENT

Try to cover the following points in a conversational manner and not necessarily in the order listed:

Name

Where They Can Be Reached (Home or business phone number, or address, if they have no phone.)

Age (Many people are touchy about giving their age, so if it matters to you, tell them what age bracket you prefer and ask if they fit into it.)

Sex

Occupation

Type of Current Living Situation (for example, family, group household, living alone, etc.)

Reason They Are Looking For a Change of Residence

Ability to Pay First and Last Months' Rent and a Security Deposit

Any Children?

Pets (Do they have any? Are they willing to live with yours?)

Special Considerations (If you wish to exchange all or part of the rent for a service, such as baby-sitting or yard work, would they be willing to comply? Do they have any special needs or requirements that you would have to fulfill?)

Date and Time for Face-To-Face Interview

Notes, Impressions, and Comments

Phone Interview Checklist
FOR THOSE WHO ARE LOOKING FOR SPACE TO RENT

Try to cover the points listed in a conversational manner and not necessarily in the order listed. (If the lead was from a newspaper ad, staple it to the sheet.)

Name (Although people with space to share may be unwilling to provide their full names to unscreened applicants for reasons of privacy, most will be willing to give you their first name.)

How You Reached Them (phone number you called)

Location

How Big is the Room? How Much Closet Space Does it Have?

Financial Data:
Rent per month? Are utilities included?
What advance payments are necessary: first month? last month?
Security deposit?

Access to Other Areas:
Living room and/or family room? Garden?
Are kitchen privileges included?
Is there a parking space for your car?
Is there storage space included or available?

Who Else Lives There:
How many others live there? Males? Females?
How old are they? Adults? Children?
Are they family or other renters?
How many will share your bathroom?

Special Considerations (If you wish to exchange all or part of the rent for a service, would they be willing to comply? Do they have any special needs or requirements?)

Date And Time For Face-To-Face Interview

Notes, Impressions, and Comments

Face-to-Face: Listening to Your Head and Your Heart

The principle of heeding your gut reactions also holds true during face-to-face interviews. Listen to your intuitions. Ask questions, of course, and listen to the *content* of the answers, but also listen to your emotional reactions. If you find yourself feeling uneasy, uptight, or frightened in any way, take it as a warning from your innards that you and this person will probably not get along well enough to live harmoniously together.

We know of one woman who spent two hours interviewing a prospective renter in spite of her negative gut reaction to him. She finally realized that this was because of his religious beliefs, which were somewhat fanatical. After he left, her fifteen-year-old daughter, who had walked through the room during the interview, commented, "What was he, some kind of a religious nut?"

Her astonished mother responded, "Yes, he was, but how did you know? He didn't say anything about that when you were in the room, did he?"

The daughter thought about it for a moment before replying, "No, he *didn't*, but he just felt weird in a religious way—maybe it was in his voice."

The woman realized that she also had felt uneasy about the man's voice, but had discounted her feelings instead of trusting them, as her daughter had. The next time, she knew better, although it always took her much longer than her daughter to evaluate people. From then on, she tried to include her daughter in the interviewing process whenever she could.

On the other hand, if you feel warm and friendly toward a person you are interviewing, don't act on your emotions alone and throw out everything else you intended to consider. Simply take it as a good sign and proceed with the rest of the interview. It's perfectly possible to feel a great deal of warmth and friendship toward someone and for that person to turn out to be a miserable housemate anyway. So use both your head and your heart!

But what should you ask prospective housemates? How personal can you get without giving offense? When you realize that living with someone is a very personal relationship, you can see that it is not only proper to ask personal questions, but it is vitally necessary that you find out how the other person feels about many of the issues we discussed at the beginning of this chapter. It may not be necessary to cover every issue we've brought up, but do focus on the ones that matter to you the most. We suggest that you share your views on such issues as noise, children, overnight guests, and the like and that you ask them in return to tell you how they feel about such things so that you can see if you will be compatible. Don't worry about offending people—if they don't understand your need to know these things, you probably don't want to live with them anyway.

Obviously, if you have children of your own and are looking for another single parent or couple with children, it will be important for you to compare notes about your respective views on child-raising and acceptable standards of behavior. You may not agree on everything, but it is hard for one child to be severely disciplined while the other parents' kids are getting away with murder. So, your feelings and beliefs about parenting and your rules regarding your children must at least be in the same ball park. Not only that, it is also important to discuss this issue with single adults who are prospective housemates, to avoid clashes over their expectations or indulgences where your children are concerned. Minor variations are fine, but the big issues should be agreed on before the household is set up.

If you are being interviewed by people with space to rent, you might want to find out if they own the house or apartment and, if they are renting, whether they have their landlord's permission to sublet. This is also the proper time to ask why they are looking for someone to share their space.

On the other hand, if you are doing the interviewing, now is the time to ask prospective renters why they are planning to change their place of residence, if you have not already done so.

In either case, understand that you are not merely being nosy. If a person is undergoing a trial separation from a spouse and the couple reconciles, you might have to find another roommate (or another room). If someone has had trouble paying his or her previous rent (or is having trouble making mortgage payments) you might want to think seriously about their financial stability. Similarly, if he or she has not gotten along with previous roommates (or renters), this may be a danger signal.

Getting and Checking References

By all means ask for references! No matter how much you like a person, do not skip this step! Some people are enormously charming, likable, even lovable, when you first meet them, but possess a Jekyll-and-Hyde personality that can be brought on by drink, hormones, having psychological buttons pushed—or by the light of the full moon. You should always request to speak with a couple of people who have known them well, preferably for several years. You should do this even if it means making a long-distance call or two.

Ask how long they've known the person and how well. Be blunt about your need for information. Ask if there have been any financial problems that they know of, and what it's like to be in the person's company for an extended period of time. Also ask if the person has any psychological or social problems or other hang-ups. Listen closely to their answers. Even if they are obviously trying to present your applicant in as favorable a light as possible, most people tend to be honest when it comes to answering a direct question. Or they may pause and give a carefully guarded reply if there is something negative they'd rather not say. This is the time to push a bit further, to ask another question about the same thing, or to say, "I noticed you hesitated there. Does that mean that there may be a drinking problem (or whatever)?" Often, faced with such a candid question, people will break down and say, "Well, yes, I didn't want to say anything, but Fred drinks quite a bit." If you do get negative feedback, and you really like the applicant and feel that things might work out anyway, be sure to raise the question when you meet again. If necessary, ask applicants for additional references until you feel satisfied that they are who they say they are.

It is wise to ask to be put in touch with your applicant's former landlord or roommates. These people can not only tell you what the person was like to live with, and in what condition he or she maintained the property, but they will also probably know if your prospective housemate was financially stable.

Whether you are renting out space or looking for a place to live, you must be ready to provide references about yourself. Remember, the person you are talking to is in exactly the same position as you are with regard to taking the risk of living with a stranger. So have a list of people you have already been in touch with who have said that they are willing to give references for you. *Never* just give someone a list of names without first checking with those people—they might love you enormously, but perhaps their dog just died and they are not in the mood to talk to anyone. If your prospective housemate calls and gets turned off, it might create a bad impression of you that was entirely erroneous.

We also suggest that you ask to speak to the personnel department where the applicant works, or to his or her immediate superior, and ask for a bank reference, as well. Most banks will refuse to provide you with the exact balance in someone's account, but they may tell you how many digits long it is. There are excellent credit bureaus that can provide you with information regarding the person's credit history, but in some cases, you must have the proper credentials to obtain it.

It may not be fun to play detective, but it is always better to be the sleuth than the victim! If you take the time and trouble to follow this process, you will be going a long way toward making sure that your final choice will be a good one.

If you find someone you think you might like to live with, but one of you is not totally sure you'll be compatible, it is perfectly acceptable to suggest spending a trial weekend, or even a longer period, together. (This works best when there is no furniture-moving involved.) Be very precise about the length of that period, and give all parties concerned the right to cancel before then if they aren't happy.

One final note. When you have made your choice, try to contact the other finalists to tell them that, at least for the present, they will not be living with you. It has always seemed rude to us when someone said, "I'll make my decision soon and let you know," and never bothered to call to say, "Sorry, it didn't work out." Even if you are not bothered by your conscience on this one, there is always the possibility that Mr. or Ms. Right will turn out to be wrong, and it is nice to have a couple of "also-rans" to fall back on.

The next step, before the person moves in, is to agree on how the housekeeping responsibilities will be split. In the next chapter, we'll tell you how to do this with a minimum of hassle.

CHAPTER III

How to Give Everyone a Piece of the Action

It has been said that a large proportion of marriages break up over one of two major factors: money and sex. Although a group household is very much like a marriage, the crucial factors are somewhat different. Although sex may still turn out to be an issue (and we'll get to that in chapter VII) the critical issue that can make or break a group household is sharing, especially as it applies to money, chores, and space.

In a marriage, money problems usually revolve around who will provide it and how it will be spent. In a group household, it is much more likely to be a question of whether an individual is paying a fair share of the expenses and whether he or she is paying them on time. The same difference applies to household chores: In a traditional marriage, the various chores went with the sexual roles—the wife shopped and cooked and sewed and cleaned the house, while the husband was responsible for paying the bills, fixing whatever wore out or broke down, and keeping the yard and the car in order. Although these jobs may be distributed differently in modern marriages, with the gourmet husband doing most of the cooking and the wife fixing the car, the tasks usually belong to one member of the family or the other. In a group household, however, such tasks are usually shared, with each member of the household taking a turn at each one of the jobs. This is not a cut-and-dried rule, as we will see, but if arrangements aren't clearly defined, a lot of trouble can ensue. And when it comes to space, clear agreements are just as crucial, especially when several people are sharing relatively limited amounts of it. There have probably been more fights over medicine cabinets and storage space than there have been over the vast deserts in the Middle East!

Whether it is a marriage or a group household that is in conflict, the answer is the same: communication— preferably before conflicts have a chance to occur, and definitely after trouble is already brewing. Reaching agreement about what each person's share of the expenses, work, and space will be *before* you move in together is a lot easier than simply moving a bunch of relative strangers and their possessions into a confined space and attempting to split the resources and responsibilities on a he-who-grabs-first-and-can-hang-on-to-it-keeps-it basis. When conflicts occur, as they inevitably will, you will find that having set up procedures to express and resolve your differences will make the difference between a general free-for-all and a harmonious solution, in most cases. In a later chapter, "A Family of Friends," we talk about a proper setting for reaching those agreements and provide a sample Household Agreement to aid you in creating one that suits the particular needs of your household.

Obviously, if you are the owner of the home in question, you will be in a position of strength when it comes to the way the house will be run. But remember that although you have selected your potential housemates and can get rid of them if they fail to be compatible with your life-style, you still have a large stake in keeping the members of the household happy. If they leave in a huff (or any other vehicle) you are the one who will be stuck with all the bills until new renters can be found to help pay them.

As we mentioned in chapter II, most of the people who decide to create a group household are either financially motivated or looking for companionship, or both. Therefore, before coming to a decision as to how much you wish to charge someone to share your space, be very clear on your priorities. Do you need to charge as much as you can in order to keep your finances in order? Or would you rather have a compatible person with a relatively limited income do a larger share of the work around the house as part of his or her monthly contribution?

A Good Support System Can Be the Key to a Successful Career!

As many of us have found out the hard way, a house can be a mixed blessing. It can be a wondrous shelter, a castle filled with space for treasures and privacy—or it can be a demanding tyrant with a neverending list of chores and responsibilities. To paraphrase several boat owners: A house can be a hole in the ground into which you must pour an endless supply of work and money. Deanna was confronted with this paradox a couple of years ago, and we believe her story may be of benefit to those of you who face similar problems:

When Deanna moved herself and her young son, Casey, to Santa Barbara, she felt that she finally had it made. Her first book was on the stands and earning enough in royalties to allow her to live modestly until she could write another. She even thought she could afford to buy a house. She had added up what it had been costing her each month to rent an apartment to live in and a studio to work in, to drive back and forth to work, to eat lunch out, and to pay for a housekeeper who kept an eye on her son after school and kept the place clean and the clothes washed. Then, with the aide of her parents, a real estate agent who possessed the imagination and hidden powers of a fairy godmother, and an optimistic bank who owed her real estate agent a couple of favors, she found a house in which to live and work for little more than her previous monthly expenses. The difference was made up by the tax advantages of owning a home and taking a business deduction on the portion of it that she used for work. Now all she had to do was settle down and write that next book . . .

. . . and clean the house,
. . . and do the wash,
. . . and pick her son up after school and take him to the dentist,
. . . and do the gardening,
. . . and fix the car and anything else that broke,
. . . and strip the previous owner's wild wallpaper off the walls,
. . . and pay the bills.

But how could she pay the bills if she didn't complete another book? And how could she complete another book if she had no time or energy left after doing all of the above? It seemed like an endless circle of frustration.

"How did I ever get so dumb?" she asked herself. "By being determined to be self-sufficient, self-supporting, and self-actualized I have managed to go full circle and become a housewife again. But this time, I'm tied to a house that is draining my life away, with no husband to bring home the money to support the family or mow the lawn or fix the car or do the chores on weekends, in accordance with the Great American Life-style I was so glad to leave behind. And, to make matters worse, at the same time I've managed to become a small business owner with no secretary, no bookkeeper, no assistants to run errands and do the Mickey Mouse stuff, and—what is worse—no 'little woman' at home to take care of the kids, cook me dinner, iron my shirts, or keep the home fires burning while I'm away on business! By freeing myself from traditional roles, I've placed myself in a position where I can't fulfill any one of them satisfactorily. I've managed to saddle myself with the traditional responsibilities of both sexes and the traditional advantages of neither. I'm turning into a lousy, harassed mother; an inefficient housekeeper and homeowner; and with all the pressure and responsibility, I haven't been able to find time to write a coherent line in months. If this keeps up, I won't be able to support myself at all and everything will just go down the drain."

The future looked black indeed.

Then into Deanna's life came an efficiency expert who specialized in personal matters. Instead of going into the offices and factories of large corporations and telling them where they were wasting time and money and how to fix it, this man would move into people's homes and live with them for a week or so, taking careful note of what went on there and listening to everyone's complaints and needs and goals and dreams. Then he would help them to restructure their lives so they could get what they wanted. He came into Deanna's home as a guest, but once he saw her dilemma, he couldn't resist giving her some professional advice.

First, he had her make a list of everything she had to do. Every chore and task, every facet of work and home life, and everything she wanted to do, whether or not she currently had the time to do it. The list went on for pages. There were hundreds of items on it. When she finished adding the last item, Deanna looked at it in horrified disbelief. No wonder she was anxious, depressed, irritable, and blocked creatively—there wasn't a soul on earth who could manage to find the time to do all those things, let alone do them properly! "I'm on a treadmill to nowhere," she wailed. "How do I get off?—And who'll pick up the pieces if I do?"

The efficiency expert smiled. "That's the next step," he assured her and set her to work on her list again. "I want you to look at each item and decide what kind of person you would need to do that job for you. Make a little code for each kind of person or talent: G for gardener or handyperson, S for secretary, H for housekeeper, etc. If no one but you can do a job, or if it is something you want to do yourself because it gives you great pleasure, put a D for Deanna next to it. If part of a job can be done by someone else with your backup or supervision, put both codes next to it. Then we'll go through the list and figure out just who and what you need to lighten and share your load."

"But how could I pay these people?" she wanted to know.

"Later," he said. "One step at a time."

When the coding was done, Deanna found that it would take the following people to handle all her tasks and responsibilities, so that she could have the time to do the traveling and writing that were necessary for her to earn a living: a housekeeper who could keep the house clean, wash the clothes, do the shopping, cook dinner, and stay with her son when Deanna was out of town; a handyperson capable of maintaining and repairing the car and the house and grounds; and a secretary/assistant who could take care of the filing, the correspondence, and run errands around town.

"Terrific," Deanna thought, looking over the list. "Anyone could do anything with a housekeeper and handyperson and a secretary." Then it occurred to her that most people of her age and accomplishments who owned their own businesses did have exactly that kind of support system: at least one assistant to do the office work and errands—and usually a maintenance person or an "office boy" as well! (How many executives got down and scrubbed the office floor and toilet at the end of the day?) And a wife or housekeeper at home. Plus the services of gardeners, mechanics, and other maintenance people as needed! How unrealistic it had been for her to assume that she could do it all herself! And then she thought of all the other divorced mothers she knew who were trying to do the same futile thing. Maybe that was something men had learned in all their years in the business world that women were just catching on to: You couldn't amount to anything without a support system. It took proper support to supply the time and energy one needed to exercise enough creativity and intelligence to succeed. Without it, you didn't stand a chance.

Fine. It all made sense. But how was she going to find the money to pay for such a support team? The treadmill seemed to grind on as inexorably as ever. The efficiency expert seemed quite unperturbed by her dilemma. "Well, my dear," he said, eyeing her with amusement, "the answer lies—as most creative solutions do—outside of the box you've drawn in your mind. You have been thinking in traditional terms where people get paid for their support in either love and security or money. There are other things that people need, you know. And, although you are currently a bit short of cash, you do have considerable assets of other kinds to offer." Deanna stared at him blankly, wondering if she should take offense. What exactly did he have in mind?

"You have this house. A haven, I may say, that would be a rich reward for anyone. You have a guest room, I believe, convenient to the kitchen and the downstairs bath. Don't you think such a room would be of value to someone?"

"Sure," she replied, "but I couldn't rent it out for enough to pay the people I need even minimum wages and I'd have the burden of a tenant on top of everything else."

"Why not trade it?" he asked.

"To whom?" Deanna wanted to know. "If you trade a live-in housekeeper room and board in return for full-time housekeeping, she generally wants at least $600 per month in wages, as well. And I'd still need an assistant and a handyperson."

"What about someone who could do all three kinds of jobs?"

"Even if I could find someone who was willing and able to do all those things in exchange for room and board, they would have no time to do anything else," she replied. "Anyone with a job could never do all that stuff as well. I learned that the hard way! And why would anyone want to spend most of their time around here, just in return for room and board?"

Deanna's friend smiled gently. "To learn," he said, "to learn from you. You do have other assets, you know."

Here we go again! she thought.

"Yes," he continued. "In your interesting life you have learned many things, many skills, that would be quite valuable to someone who was just starting out in life. A student, for instance, who wanted to benefit from all your experience, listen to your intelligent ideas, try out his or her skills under your guidance, and have a lovely place to live as well. You are only a few blocks from the college, you know, and there would be time for an energetic student to take classes there as well. A kind of work-study program, you see."

"And you really think that such a person exists?" Deanna asked doubtfully.

"As far as I'm concerned, if such a person did not already exist, you could create one," was the answer. "All you really have to do is be very clear on what you want; that's where the magic really lies. The rest is simply believing it is possible, and willing it to happen—Oh, and doing everything you can to help make it happen."

"Like what?" Deanna wanted to know. There had to be some way to bring this out of the realm of metaphysics and into reality.

"You could check out the college and university employment programs, and tell everyone you meet that you are looking for someone. And be open-minded and give the person a chance when he or she turns up. You never get exactly what you expect, you know."

The rest is history, as they say. Within two months, Deanna was invited to go to Colorado on business. A friend who heard that she needed someone to look after her son while she was gone mentioned that his younger brother was about to move into town to attend college there. He had intelligence, boundless energy, and absolutely no money. Would she be willing to let him stay at her home with her son while she was gone? He was a lovely kid, and it would give him some time to get his bearings, find a part-time job, and enroll in classes. The young man, whose name was John, came to stay on a trial basis. He turned out to be a very likable fellow. At twenty-one, he seemed like a model older brother to her sixteen-year-old son and quite trustworthy. Deanna went off happily to Colorado, decided to treat herself to a couple of days of skiing when her work was over; tore the ligaments in her knee; and limped home unable to walk, drive, or do practically anything.

"I can't leave you in this mess," said John, "I guess I'd better stay on a while and take care of things."

By the time Deanna's leg healed, John had proved to be a valuable aide indeed. Because he had worked as a mechanic, he was able to fix the truck when it broke down and tune the car as well. He was willing and able to keep after the house, and Casey found that he preferred to do a share of the chores rather than loaf around while his newfound friend did all the work. John knew enough from the after-school jobs he'd held to be able to paint the deck and fix the appliances when they broke. After some trial and error and a couple of cooking lessons, he also turned out to be a pretty good cook. Soon he was doing most of the food shopping and other errands around town as well.

During her enforced convalescence, Deanna found herself so free to write that she soon had enough commissions for articles and books to be able to get herself a computer, which she used for word processing.

John considered himself well rewarded: He could never have afforded to live so well or eat so heartily on his own. He loved working on vehicles and now had a car at his disposal. He was delighted at the prospect of learning organic gardening, and Deanna not only had a plot of land in the backyard that she had been composting for a year but also had the information, the tools, and a whole crew of organic farmer friends to help him gain the practical knowledge he needed. By the end of summer he had put in a garden that was producing enough organic vegetables to substantially reduce the household food bills. He was learning skills that would more than pay off when he had a place of his own to look after. He had come to a strange city and found a home that teemed with interesting people and newfound friends. But the biggest payoff for him was Deanna's new computer. Since he was a computer programming and electrical engineering major, having access to a computer at home was an unimaginable joy and creative opportunity. In gratitude, John created a program that kept track of Deanna's expenses. Each month, he entered her checks and credit card statements and her cash receipts and ended up with a statement that broke them down into tax categories—which saved her money in accountant's fees at the end of the year.

In general, the experience proved equally valuable to both of them. For example, in return for the use of the hot tub, he cleaned it and kept the filter and pump in good condition. There seemed to be no limit to the exchange of opportunities and rewards for both of them.

For as long as John lived with her, Deanna was delighted with the arrangement. He was a younger brother to her and an older brother to Casey. "Living with John had all the advantages of 'having a man around the house' with none of the emotional wear and tear," she says. "John was a free-standing individual. He had his friends and social life and I had mine. There was no jealousy, no dependency, no role-playing in our relationship. We always felt that there was a very fair exchange of services and rewards between us, and John's example made Casey more productive and responsible as well. At that time I couldn't have asked for a better solution to my problems."

Splitting Up the Rent

Whether you own the place or are just the one who initiated setting up the household, because you are the "prime mover" of the establishment, you are going to have to decide how much space to offer and how much rent to charge for it before you can begin the search for housemates.

No matter what your priorities, it is important to begin by finding out how much the space you have to offer is worth at current rates. You can do this by reading the "Rooms for Rent" and "Roommates Wanted" columns in your local papers and by consulting rental and roommate agencies to see what similar space in neighborhoods like yours is going for. Keep the following factors in mind when comparing the listings to what you have to offer:

- How large is the room?
- Is there a private bathroom?
- Is the location similar to yours in prestige, convenience, or current rental rates?
- Is it in a private house or an apartment?
- Is the use of the kitchen included? The living areas? The garden?
- Is parking provided?
- Does the rent include utilities?
- How many other people will share the premises?

Even when all these factors are equal, there is still usually quite a "spread" between the lowest and highest rent for similar property. How you decide what you must charge for your space depends on whether you own the house or are simply splitting up a house or apartment you are renting from someone else, so let's tackle each of these cases separately.

If You Want to Share Rented Space

The easiest way to figure out what to charge for rooms in an apartment or house you are already renting is to divide the rent you are currently paying by as many people as you would like to have in your household. In this way, each of you will end up paying an equal share. However, there are circumstances where this simple procedure will not work.

For instance, if one member of the household is going to end up with a large master bedroom and a private bath, while the others will have to make do with smaller rooms and a shared bath, the person with the most luxurious quarters should be willing to pay a premium for them. If parking spaces go with the rental, those who will have the use of them should also pay more than those who are going to have to park on the street. As initiator of the household, you have every right to retain the best accommodations, but if you would rather save money, you can allocate them to the member of the household who is willing to pay the largest proportion of the rent.

Of course, if you are lucky enough to be paying a low rent for a fairly nice house or apartment, there may be nothing to stop you from simply charging the highest going rate for the rooms you wish to rent and walking away with a tidy profit each month. That's the wonderful law of supply and demand in action. However, before you decide to go this route, check the sublet clause of your lease extra carefully to be sure that you are allowed to sublet space. Your landlords may be even less enthusiastic about your making a profit on their property than they will be about your subletting it at all. Also, be sure that your tenant, (or housemates) are aware of what you are doing. By being up-front about the fact that you are charging them the current fair price for the space they are renting and are taking them into your home because you need the extra money to keep your finances in order, you will avoid being attacked by disillusioned roommates who had assumed that you were paying the same share of the rent as they were.

If You Own the House

If you own the house, potential housemates will probably assume that you are making a profit on the situation, and that you will expect to keep the master suite and the parking for yourself. When one person owns the property, an equitable split of the expenses is not as ticklish a point as it is when you are all renting space from someone else. Of course, you may also be quite willing to relinquish the most luxurious quarters in your home to someone who is willing to pay a good price for them. It's up to you. But before you decide which space to rent and how much to charge for it, estimate your monthly house-related expenses to see what the place is costing you. Do this by adding up the following items:

- Monthly mortgage payment
- Property taxes (divide by 12 if you pay them yearly)
- Homeowner's insurance (divide by 12 if you pay yearly)
- Sanitation services
- Garden or pool maintenance charges each month (Include these in your initial figures even if you want to trade these services for part of the rent.)
- Cable television service
- Any other monthly home maintenance expenses *except* water, gas, electricity, telephones, and any other utilities or services that are based on consumption.

The resulting figure is the "nut" or basic monthly cost of maintaining your home. As the owner, you can decide what you feel you deserve to get in return for the money you've invested in the house and the responsibility and expense of repainting and repairing it over the years.

"You Light Up My Life—and You Should Pay for It!"

Although many people choose to rent space to others on a utilities-included basis, we have found that this is not a very good idea for a couple of reasons. First, taking an average of what you've spent each month in the past for gas, electricity, water, etc., and adding it to the estimate of monthly expenses on which you base your rental figures is useless, since those bills will go up as soon as there are more occupants using the services. Not only that, if you include these utilities in your rent, you are going to have to raise the rent every time the cost of those services goes up or bear the brunt of the increases yourself. When you realize that the cost of gas and electricity has increased 200 to 300 percent in the past year or two and continues to rise in leaps and bounds, you can see that any rental that includes utilities as a fixed item is going to prove less and less equitable or profitable and will have to be renegotiated frequently.

Whether you own the house or are sharing it with other renters, it is a much better idea to require them to pay their share as soon as the bills come in each month. Since utility companies follow tight billing schedules, it shouldn't be difficult for everyone to anticipate when those bills will arrive and to arrange to have the money on hand in time to pay them without incurring late-payment charges. If anyone does hold up payment by not anteing up his or her share on time, the late payment charges should be tacked on to that person's share of the next month's bill. If the situation continues, find a new roommate!

Just what each one's share should be is another matter. In most cases, you can simply split the gas, water, and electricity bills equally unless one or more of you uses a disproportionate share. Anyone who works at home will certainly consume more utilities than someone who leaves early in the morning and doesn't return until evening. The same goes for such personal electrical appliances as air conditioners, water beds, TVs and stereos, electric typewriters, sewing machines, and home computers. Anyone who uses items such as these to a much greater extent than the rest of the household should be prepared to pay a larger share of the electric bill. The electric company is quite willing to provide a meter at no cost that can tell you exactly how much current a particular appliance uses. You simply plug the appliance into the meter and plug the meter into the wall to measure the amount of current that passes through the cord. A week of metering is usually sufficient for the power company to be able to tell you what percentage of the monthly household current is being used by a particular appliance.

Please realize that, apart from these extreme cases, most households find that consumption of all utilities seems to average out in the long run and that it is much easier to simply divide the bills equally. Mike may take extra-long showers, Mary may do four washes a week, Dora may sit in the hot tub for hours, and Fred may play his stereo constantly; but in the end all of their idiosyncrasies will probably cancel each other out. So when it comes to splitting up the bills, or anything else for that matter, remember: *Keep it fair but keep it simple!*

"WHO MADE THAT PHONE CALL TO FAIRBANKS, ALASKA?"

There are several things to consider when it comes to deciding what to do about telephone service. The cheapest way to go is for everyone to use one telephone number, split the basic monthly charge (which can include separate phonebook and information listings at a very low cost), and pay for his or her own long-distance calls through individual long-distance services. Anyone who prefers privacy and instant access to the phone can have his or her own private phone line installed and pay for it on an individual basis. Be sure to ask whether the telephone company in your area offers a discount on the basic monthly charges for the additional private lines at your address. Telephone companies in certain areas of the country offer a third alternative: billing more than one phone line and number as though they were one phone and charging less for the service than it would if they had to bill each phone individually. Members of group households with this service can simply split the monthly charge and pay for long-distance calls individually.

You Can Save Money on Phone Service

No matter how you choose to arrange things, you will always save money if you can have all the phones lines and extensions set up during the same service call. And now that you can buy telephone cords, jacks, and telephones at discount prices in a wide variety of stores, new members of the household who choose to share an already existing line and number can furnish their own equipment and hook up their extensions themselves without incurring any extra charges from the telephone company for installation, jacks, or instruments.

Don't Let "Teleburglers" Terrorize Your Home!

To avoid those "mystery phone calls" that seem to crop up on the bills of the most harmonious households, all those who share a phone should list each long-distance call they initiate in a household telephone log *as soon as each call is completed*. Each entry should include the date, the time (*when* the call was made, not how long it lasted), and the number called. If you like, the telephone log can be incorporated in a "Bible" that may not save souls but will certainly save time, trouble, and tempers.

THE BIBLE: KEEPING TRACK OF EXPENSES

All of the items we've covered so far have one thing in common: Sooner or later, all the adult members of your household are going to have to come up with their share of the expenses and they are going to have to come up with them on time. The best way to avoid misunderstandings, lame excuses, and other end-runs around bill paying is to keep careful track of expenses as they occur. An expense log (known in some households as the "Bible") should be kept where everyone can get at it, and one person should be responsible for listing each bill as it comes in. The "Keeper of the Bible" should also be responsible for paying the bills. Although this job can be assigned on a rotating basis, most houses run more smoothly if one person handles it over a long period of time. In return for taking on this detailed and time-consuming job, the Keeper of the Bible should be excused from those special once-a-month cleanup chores we'll get to later in this chapter. Of course, if you own the house, or are the person in whose name the accounts have been established, you will probably want to assume this responsibility permanently, whether or not you get out of washing the windows. After all, you have the most motivation to see to it that the bills are paid!

Keep a separate page for each member of the household and break it down to show the amount of the bill, the amount the person owes, and when the money is due for each item. Make the due date a week ahead of the actual deadline to allow time for collection and payment. Here's a page from the "Bible" for one member of a typical group household:

PETER PAYFAST:

Item	Pay To	Total Charges	Your Share	Due Date	Date Paid
February rent	H. K.		$300.00	1/25	1/23
Electricity	H. K.	$43.36	14.44	2/3	2/3
Gas	H. K.	30.33	10.11	2/6	2/3
Telephone	H. K.	90.27	18.04	2/8	2/3
Loan from Mike	M. R.	25.00	25.00	ASAP!	2/3
Household supplies	M. R.	46.00	15.34	2/1	2/3
Booze for party	P. P.	33.00	11.00	2/15	(H:pd M:no)
March rent	H. K.		$300.00	2/25	
Electricity	H. K.	49.49	46.47	3/3	
Present for Kathy	M. R.	25.97	12.98	3/10	

Such a record helps housemates keep track of what they owe and to whom they owe it. It is up to the people who pay out money to keep track of who has not paid them back. And it is up each person to be sure that his or her payment is duly recorded in the "Bible." In the above illustration, Peter can look at his page to see if he is keeping up with his debts and can also remind himself that, although he has received Mike's share of money he laid out for the party refreshments, he still hasn't been repaid by Helen.

PREVENTING LAST-MINUTE PROBLEMS

To prevent problems and misunderstandings when people move out of your household, we suggest that—unless there are extenuating circumstances that you can accept—all incoming members should be required to provide the first and last month's rent and a cleaning and security deposit before they move in. There are many reasons why this procedure pays off for everyone concerned, and we get into them in detail in the last chapter of this book. If you can't wait to know these reasons, we won't mind if you skip ahead and read that section now. It begins on page 216.

JOINT HOUSEHOLD CHECKING ACCOUNTS

If almost all the basic expenses are split evenly in your household, you might want to simplify matters by opening a joint checking account in which each of the members of the household can deposit his or her share of the estimated monthly expenses plus a little extra to cover the unexpected. Judging from the household expenses

illustrated above, Mike, Pete. ...
agree to deposit $370 per mont.
electricity, basic household supp.
tainment. If a surplus builds up, the
it equally or throw themselves a big pa
develops each will ante up an equal addi

Although joint checking may have its adv.
full of pitfalls for unstable, unwary, or inefficic... ...e-
holds. Please note that such an account should ...y be
used for basic expenses and *never* for such personally
fluctuating items as long-distance phone calls or personal expenses, loans, or gifts. Unless you are very, very
rigid about only using it for paying *equally divided* bills,
a joint account can cause problems. The checkbook
should be the responsibility of one person (the same one
responsible for the "Bible," of course) and this type of
arrangement should only be set up by well-established
households whose members have proved their reliabil-
ity over a period of time.

Sharing Space: How to Divide and Conquer

There are several types of space involved here: living
space, storage space, closet space, parking space, cabinet
and shelf space in the kitchen and bathroom, and space
to exhibit and enjoy your favorite pieces of furniture or
works of art. The two Golden Rules for all of these space
cases are (1) Let each have a fair share and (2) Never
give up anything for nothing!

Unless you are simply renting out bedroom, bath, and
kitchen privileges in a house you own, every member
of a group household should have the use of an equitable
and adequate portion of the place in which to use and
store personal effects. Even if one person is paying a

are of the rent for the master bedroom and bath, or she should be aware that the money is going for exactly that, and not for a disproportionate share of the rest of the space in the house, unless special arrangements were part of the original bargain.

Please notice that we specified "equitable and *adequate*." Over years of sharing everything from dormitory rooms to large homes with other people, we've found again and again that, just as in large cities, most controversies in group households arise from overcrowding. Most people, including those who are happily married, require a room where they can retreat to be alone with their own thoughts and silences. Anyone who has attempted to share a one-room apartment with a friend or mate has found this out before very long. Although we'll get into the entire issue of privacy later in the book, we want to make the point here that it is extremely unwise to form a group household that involves any single individual's sharing bedrooms unless they are small children. What's more, there must be adequate closet space, storage space, and shelf space for all housemembers to have easy access to the things they use daily and a safe place for the long-term storage of special things that they cannot bear to part with.

The initiator of a group household must make a survey of the space available and have a good idea of how it can be divided and how many people it can accommodate, before beginning the process of locating and selecting housemates. Be sure that all serious candidates for your new "family" are shown the amount and location of the closets, cabinets, and shelves they can expect to use and that they consider it adequate for their needs *before* you close the deal and allow them to move in. To prevent them from showing up with an eleven-foot sofa or thirty cases of books and records, be sure to ask them during the initial interview if they have any possessions that may not fit into the house or apartment easily.

Be aware that "equitable" does not always have to mean "equal." As rule 2 implies, if your entire literary life revolves around the daily paper, it is perfectly all right to relinquish your share of the bookshelves to a bookworm roommate in return for some of his or her closet space in which to keep your ski equipment. To prevent chaos, this kind of trading should be on a one-to-one basis, and if a roommate leaves, everyone who has traded space with that person should renegotiate with the new member of the extended family so that the new roommate can start off with a fair share of the house.

WHERE TO PUT AUNT ADDIE'S CHAIR

As the newspaper columns will tell you, living space comes in two flavors: furnished and unfurnished. In either case, there are certain items that are basic and vital to life, and there are a lot that vary according to individual tastes and circumstances.

What, then, should new housemates be expected—and allowed—to bring with them? Generally speaking, individual roommates should be prepared to furnish their own:

- Towels and toilet articles
- Pillows, sheets, and blankets
- TVs, stereos, typewriters, etc., for personal use
- Dishes and cooking utensils—if the existing household lacks enough for everyone

If you are entering a group household in a furnished house or apartment, there is probably enough furniture already, and this may present some problems if you have furniture of your own to deal with. The precious possessions that you pinched your pennies to buy, wrested from the combat of divorce, or were awarded posthumously by favorite relatives may be greeted with joy— "We really needed a harpsichord!"—or with disdain— "Why did you frame your dirty linen?" To avoid trouble, be sure that there is room for your additions, and that they suit everyone's taste *before* you move in. If you cannot survive without Aunt Addie's chair, and it is too large to fit into the bedroom you will inhabit, be sure to ask whether it can be placed in the general living space while you are still in the negotiating stage so that you and/or the chair can choose to reside elsewhere if necessary. If you acquire something after you're already established in the house that will fit neither your hope chest nor your room, you can use a family meeting (we talk about them later in "A Family of Friends") to gain approval for placing it in the general living space, at least on a trial basis. Getting turned down may rankle if the members of your extended family fail to see the charm of your dearest aunt's cherished heirloom, but you may feel better when they also reject someone else's glass-enclosed collection of reptiles!

If you are the initiator of a group household in a house or apartment you've already furnished, you can prevent such problems by establishing a rule ahead of time that all those who want to contribute additional furniture or decorations must either be prepared to keep the stuff in their own rooms or should make certain that you and the existing members of the household are prepared to live with their possessions on an intimate basis. Otherwise, personal effects that do not fit the taste and space limitations of the house must be stored elsewhere or disposed of in some other manner, with no guilt trips or emotional operas.

On the other hand, people who are sharing unfurnished houses and apartments are usually genuinely grateful for additions to the household's meager supply of furniture and appliances. So if Aunt Addie has left you not just a chair but a houseful of Chippendale, or if you've been awarded most of the furniture and a collection of gourmet cooking utensils in lieu of alimony, look for or initiate a group household in an unfurnished abode. The other members may even allow you to pay less rent in return for furnishing the place for them!

COMMUNITY PROPERTY

If your household lacks a comfortable sofa, a toaster, a vacuum cleaner, or some other item necessary to the happiness of all concerned, should the members of the household buy one in common? Because old sofas never die, while roommates fade away, such arrangements frequently cause hassles when it is time for someone to leave. It may be difficult to find a roommate who will come up with the money for an expensive appliance knowing that everyone is going to share it, so buying it together may be the only thing to do. But be sure that everyone is in agreement as to how that item will be treated when one of its owners is on the way out of the extended family. If it is something relatively inexpensive, like a toaster or a juicer, the roommates should each contribute an equal amount toward the purchase with the knowledge that it now belongs to the house and will remain there as long as there is a household going on. If you are all going your separate ways and the household is breaking up completely, communal items can be auctioned off (with the proceeds split equally or used to throw one last party together) or you can draw lots for them.

If the item is something very expensive, such as a sofa or a television set, it is better to find a relatively cheap one secondhand, since no one wants to invest a lot of money in something that will have to be left behind. A roommate who is willing to pay $400 for a color TV for the living room might charge each of the three other people in the house $5 a month for the privilege of using it and use the money to pay the monthly installments on the set. Needless to say, this can only be done with the complete agreement of every adult member of the household, since it is just plain silly to expect someone to never sit on a sofa or watch a television simply because they haven't paid to use it. After the set is paid off, the monthly rentals should cease and the item should be treated as the property of the person who bought it and shared with the other members of the household. If the buyer moves before the item is paid off, he or she keeps the item and is stuck with the unpaid balance of the payments. If one of the other roommates moves before paying off his or her share of the item, the buyer should absorb that portion of the unpaid costs, rather than increasing the size or duration of the payments of the other roommates. (A deal is a deal!) That is the price one pays for being able to leave home with something that everyone else has helped to pay for.

FACING THE GREAT BATHROOM CHALLENGE

Aside from the kitchen (which has so many requirements and pitfalls that we've devoted an entire chapter to it), the bathroom is probably the room that generates the most household feuds. Here, competition is keen—for space, for time, for hot water. In the john, personal habits that may not rankle in other parts of the house can swiftly become incitements to riot. It is one thing to have a house-mate whose bedroom door discreetly hides a devas-tating mess. It is quite another to encounter that same filth and chaos every time you head for a quiet bath or meditation in the communal WC. Many households make wiping the sink free of water and washing out the tub mandatory every time they are used. The same goes for water on the floor. Those who fail to clean up after themselves are subjected to everything from shunning to nasty remarks at cocktail parties.

To avoid confusion and disorder, everyone who is sharing a bathroom should have an equal, adequate, and predetermined amount of space in the medicine chest or on the shelves in which to stow his or her possessions. When each person leaves the room, all cosmetics, deo-dorants, and shaving and hair-styling equipment should be put away and the decks cleaned and cleared for the next roommate's entry. If there is a shortage of space, try the following remedies:

- Agree to share one hair dryer, Water-Pik, or sun lamp. Store the extras or rotate them so everyone's gets used.
- Build extra shelves or cabinets to accommodate the load.
- Ask roommates to keep their toilet articles in their bedrooms and to bring them to the bathroom only when they need them.

Bathroom Traffic Jams: Avoiding the Unavoidable

Those of us who have been forced to commute to work in major urban areas are painfully aware of the unique combination of panic, frustration, and helplessness that can engulf us when we find the route to our daily work (and daily bread!) blocked, day after day, by other people crowding the same paths to the same goals. Since humankind in all its eons of evolution has not produced an individual who can arrive at work bright-eyed and clear-headed without a trip to the bathroom, many extended families who otherwise manage to live together in perfect harmony find themselves locked in mortal combat in the hall outside the bathroom every morning. Is this any way to run a household? You bet it isn't! But what exactly can be done about it? Finding the answer to this question has probably involved more time and talk than the search for the Holy Grail. The answer is that there isn't any good answer—just a couple of suggestions that may or may not work for you:

- If you are a collection of rich singles who bought a house together for the fun of it, build another bathroom. Better yet, build two. You might even want to include a sauna and a Jacuzzi!
- As a communal project, hang additional mirrors, build extra shelves and/or cabinets in the hall or in people's rooms, and encourage (or force) everyone to do their primping, grooming, makeup, and blow-drying *outside* the bathroom during the rush hours.
- At a family meeting, ascertain each individual's estimated time of departure for work or school and negotiate, cajole, beg, and bully each other into working out a bathroom timetable that everyone can handle. This may mean changing wakeup routines and combining schedules—for example, one person can cook breakfast while another shaves and then can use the bathroom while the shaver does the dishes. If you can keep your sense of humor, a wonderful variety of colorful and creative alternatives may emerge. Remember: Necessity is the mother of invention.

Traditionally, Saturday nights can also turn communal bathrooms into battlefields, and the members of your household may want to make it a practice to post advance warnings when they know that they will want an hour or two to prepare for a heavy date, or simply to sit in a hot tub of water and bubble their blues away. Properly handled, sharing a bathroom can provide greater opportunities to learn and appreciate the powers of communication, consideration, and assertiveness than years of human-potential counseling and self-actualization seminars.

A Word about Parking

Unless you are living in a mansion with a wide looping driveway and a four-car garage, parking is probably going to be a problem if more than two members of your household own vehicles. This is not necessarily a result of group living, as anyone who has lived in a traditional household with a couple of teenage kids can readily attest to. In these times of little space and many cars, most homes and apartments—if they come with parking spaces at all—rarely come with more than two. And motorcycles, bicycles, and skateboards are almost never provided for. Unless your household is well-organized in this department, you will find yourselves in endless tangles over who is blocking whom just when someone is frantically trying to make a quick getaway.

After trying to share parking in a variety of ways, we've found that the only hassle-free way to handle the issue is to assign each parking space to one particular vehicle and have everyone else park on the street. Just who gets the space can either be a matter of auctioning it off to the highest bidder (who pays a higher share of the rent for it) or allotting it on a rotating basis to each member of the household. If you are going to rotate, it is better

to h   let and allow each person to park for at
l   at a time. Trying to keep to a weekly park-
       is crazy-making for everyone concerned.
       dly time to know you've got it before you've

      r belief that the one who owns the place de-
      rst pick of the parking and that housemates who
      quested and been awarded parking spaces as a
      ion of entering the household should get to keep
      e spaces as long as they live there and are willing
      pay extra for them. It simply isn't fair to encourage
     meone to move into a situation that provides what they
need, and then take it away from them later on. If there
is competition for parking spaces, new entrants to the
house should be told where they stand on the waiting
list for spaces that have already been spoken for, or told
how often they can expect the rotating schedule to get
around to them.

SHARING THE LOAD: HOW TO DEAL OUT THE DIRTY WORK FAIRLY

One of the nicest things about shared living arrangements is that no one person has to be responsible for an
unpleasant task *all the time*. Of course, there are those
masochistic beings that are delighted to clean the toilet
and actually request the job, but many of them have other
quirks that make them too hard to live with in the long
run. So, chances are that although you may not have to
take out the garbage every day, you will have to do it
occasionally, along with cleaning the driveway, washing
the walls, etc. Just how you work things out will depend
on the individual talents and tastes of your housemates,

but there are a couple of options that can make things easier.

Here the key word is "equal." It doesn't really matter who does what as long as everyone agrees that his or her lot is no worse than anyone else's. And that goes for how you do the work as well as how it is assigned! If one person gives the cleaning only "a lick and a promise" and another scrubs everything spotless, there is going to be friction of quite another sort before long! In some cases it may be better to assign permanent garbage and yard-work duty to a roommate who just can't get the hang of polishing chrome and let someone who can make a house look like a home do the housework on a regular basis. Anyway, here are the basic alternatives you can consider:

Hire Someone Else to Do It

Since sharing a home usually reduces living expenses for all concerned, a household of working people may find that pooling their money to hire someone to clean the house, do the gardening, and/or clean the pool will more than pay for itself in extra free time and a well-earned chance to relax. You'll probably still have to co-operate on daily picking-up and dishwashing, but a big area of possible conflict will be eliminated. Most people don't care for housework, and trying to cooperate and work together on something no one likes to do can be exasperating. We know, we've tried it.

Houseworkers bring extra benefits with them, as well. Personal standards differ, and it's irksome to have a house-mate tell you that the floor is still sticky after you were sure you'd gotten it clean (or after you gave it a lick and a promise, hoping the others wouldn't notice). It isn't any fun being on the other side of the stick either: If you are planning to entertain on a certain evening and your housemate chooses that day to do a slipshod job on the kitchen, what do you say? If you complain, you may create a scene that will have the house still reverberating with bad vibes when the guests arrive. If you don't, you'll be in a bad mood anyway, whether the kitchen is filthy because of your inconsiderate roommate or because you're wiped out from cleaning the place up yourself as well as tending to the rest of the preparations for the evening. However, if the cleaning person has failed to do things properly, you can grumble and complain all you want to and get ample sympathy and maybe even a helping hand from your housemates to rectify the situation.

Because they live elsewhere, houseworkers can safely perform the role of "common enemy." They can serve as a kind of scapegoat by taking the blame for things that might otherwise cause friction among housemates, thus helping to create a sense of unity among the members of your household. They usually arrive well after the crisis is over and when everyone else is away at work, blissfully unaware of any hostility they may have engendered. You may bitch and complain to one another passionately—but all the housekeeper need see is a polite note saying, "Please clean the kitchen floor more thoroughly," or one that says, "Please call us this evening," so you can say the party's over and it's time to look for another job.

Teona once had a roommate who was constantly losing things and spent a good deal of his time searching for lost items and swearing ominously that "someone" must have moved them. After they hired a housekeeper, he began to deal with this situation by throwing up his

hands and saying, "The maid must have put it somewhere! I'll ask her when she comes in on Thursday."
Then he would happily forget the whole thing, allowing
the lost item to eventually surface of its own accord. She
doubts that he ever actually had to ask the maid about
anything, and the maid never knew that she served another function in their household that was at least as useful as cleaning up the place.

The Good Old Summer Camp Method

Write out a list of chores that must be done and decide
which should be rotated on a weekly basis and which
need only be done once a month. Then make a schedule
that shows when each member of the household is responsible for a particular chore. The easiest way to do
this will be familiar to anyone who has ever gone to summer camp. The schedules usually look like this:

DAILY OR WEEKLY CHORES	2/1–7	2/8–14	2/15–21	2/22–28
Vacuum the house	Mike	Peter	Helen	Mike
Dust the house	Peter	Helen	Mike	Peter
Wash kitchen floor and counters	Helen	Mike	Peter	Helen
Clean sink, stove, and refrigerator	Mike	Peter	Helen	Mike
Clean bathroom	Peter	Helen	Mike	Peter
Take out the garbage	Helen	Mike	Peter	Helen
Sweep the driveway	Mike	Peter	Helen	Mike
Grocery shopping	Peter	Helen	Mike	Peter
Water the plants	Helen	Mike	Peter	Helen
Mow the lawn	Mike	Peter	Helen	Mike

MONTHLY CHORES: February

Wash kitchen, bathroom, and living room windows	Mike
Wax kitchen and dining room floors	Peter
De-fingerprint walls	Helen
Trim hedges	Mike
Clean oven	Peter
Clean and defrost refrigerator	Helen

HOUSEHOLD PROJECTS

Preparing and planting veggie garden	Everyone!

Every four weeks, just change the dates at the top of the list and add new monthly chores and special projects.

In the interim, if people want to trade chores with each other, they can simply change the names to suit their mutual agreements. If the jobs and participants tend to remain fairly stable in your household, you can Xerox the basic list, leave room for unexpected tasks at the bottom, and post a fresh sheet each month.

The Chief-Cook-and-Bottle-Washer Approach

Hold a family meeting and agree on permanent responsibility for some or all of the regular household chores— if each member of the household is willing to go that route. It is unfair to force permanent bathroom duty on one individual just because the other members of the household are a passionate cook and a green-thumbed gardener. Although you will probably end up having to rotate certain chores that nobody loves, you may find that a surprising number of jobs are work to one person and play to another.

When a new roommate enters the household, the household tasks should be renegotiated at a family meeting to accommodate the talents and preferences of the newcomer. An exception to this would be if a member of the household has taken permanent responsibility for a particular chore, such as gardening, in return for a lower rental. In such cases, the work is considered part of the rent and not open for assumption by anyone else unless the person who has been doing it wishes to give it up.

Prospective roommates who will be entering a household where everyone else has a permanent task should be asked during the interviewing process if they would be willing to take on the responsibilities of the roommate they are replacing. Of course, if the answer is no and the individual is otherwise the best candidate for the household, then renegotiations will be in order at a family meeting to assign new tasks or share the ones nobody wants to deal with full-time.

All work around the house and grounds should be regarded as part of each roommate's obligation to the household, and treated as seriously as rent. Sharing such responsibilities is what makes a group household different from a rooming house that simply rents rooms to a bunch of strangers. It is the commitment to participate in caring for the environment you've all chosen to share, rather than simply living out your lives as isolated individuals, that makes group housekeeping so special.

Even though you may agree on how to split up the household tasks, individually owned pets and plants present a unique set of problems that call for additional thought and planning.

"I THINK YOUR CANARY ATE MY CAT!" OR "WHEN DID YOU WATER THE ASPIDISTRA?"

We will consider pets and plants as one issue, because to many of us our little green potted pals are as lovable and responsive a bunch of individuals as other people's animals must seem to them. And both can present problems, as well as joys, for group households. Whether you like coming home to your puppy or your poinsettia, your roommates are going to have to serve as surrogate parents whenever you don't come home—not to mention adjusting their lives to the patter of extra little feet, occasional accidents, and the tender caress of leaves that may cause rashes or sneezes to those who are allergic to them.

Like children, plants and pets are full members of every extended family no matter whom they officially belong to, and unless everyone in the house is happy about their presence, conflict is sure to occur. Children bring with them a unique and wonderful set of rewards and problems, and several chapters in this book focus on the various issues that concern them; but it is just as necessary to inform prospective housemates about the furry and leafy members of your entourage while you are still in the interview stage as it is to tell them that they will also be living with your teenage son and baby daughter if they decide to take up group housekeeping with you.

You might want to introduce your pet in person if you feel that its charms might help your case. Many people simply cannot stand anything that is confined to a cage or a bowl, so even if you simply want to keep a guinea pig, a canary, or goldfish in your room, it is still necessary to get everyone's approval—and that goes double for snakes and other reptiles, no matter how quiet and mild-mannered they really are.

Unless your pet raccoon and your new roommate fall into each other's arms like long-lost lovers, the chances are that you will have to take full responsibility for feeding, bathing, and walking any animal that belongs to you. Dog Yummies are not part of the food bill in a communal kitchen, and if Fido does a lot of barking, whining, and furniture damage you and he may find yourselves looking for new roommates quite often. Cats and birds tend to be less obstreperous, but to a person with allergies, living with most critters is as threatening to health and well-being as living next door to a nuclear plant may seem to you.

On the other hand, pets can provide the means for a creative exchange that makes everyone's life more pleasant. For example, Teona once worked out an arrangement whereby she dropped her housemate's son off at nursery school each morning on her way to work, in return for which her housemate fed her horses. Teona saved time and her housemate saved gas—and all the animals and people in the household got to know each other better.

If a housemate wants to bring a new pet into the house after the household has been established, be sure to consider the following questions at a family meeting first:

- Does your lease allow you to keep the animal on the premises?
- How much time and attention will it require? Who is going to supply it? If it must be walked, who will walk it?
- Is it housebroken?
- How much will it cost to license, to feed, and to pay for shots and medical checkups and treatments? Who will be responsible for paying the bills?
- Are you sure it is housebroken?
- Will your neighbors be pleased with the new addition to their environment or will they make trouble?
- Does it know it is housebroken?
- Will your furniture, houseplants, and yard survive the new addition? If not, who will pay for the damage?
- Has it been altered? If not, who will pay to have it fixed?

- Is anyone allergic to it?
- Can it be adopted on a trial basis? If it doesn't work out, is it returnable? Can it be unloaded on someone?

Unless everyone is satisfied with the answers, it is better to forget the little critter and adopt a houseplant instead. However, before you go off to buy a small forest, be aware that much the same issues apply to plants when it comes to personal taste and the responsibility for caring for them.

Most households will be happy to welcome your potted palm or ficus tree—after all, plants are the cheapest and trendiest furniture around, and most people thrive in the presence of growing things. But unless you've all chipped in for the leafy furniture to fill in the empty spaces or enhance the drab accoutrements of an otherwise underfurnished apartment, do not expect anyone to feel responsible for taking care of your plants but you. Your roommates may mean well, but not everyone has a green thumb or the psychic ability to pick up nonverbal pleas for water emanating from a thirsty creeping charlie. And if your only plant is a pot of African violets that resides inconspicuously in the corner of your room, do not expect your roommates to remember to water, fertilize, and talk to it regularly if you go out of town for a month. Just do your best to arrange a surrogate parent for it, wish it well, and send it loving thought messages while you're away, and maybe it will hang on until you get back. After that, be prepared to consign its soul to the Great Garden in the Sky and buy another violet. This attitude can save you a lot of heartaches and unpleasant homecomings.

Even if you find yourself living with a group of enthusiastic gardeners who are eager and willing to tend to your plants, the chances are that if you rely on the

general goodwill rather than a regular schedule and assigned responsibility, your plants will end up either over-
watered or undernourished, depending on who thought
who did what for which plant.

In any event, try to follow these guidelines when it
comes to living with and tending the animal and vege-
table members of your household:

1. If you want to keep an animal that cannot be confined or
any plants that either will not fit into your room or need the
type of light that only the public living areas of the house
can provide, be sure to request and gain approval from your
prospective roommates before you move in—just as you
would for Aunt Addie's chair.

2. If you tend to travel a good deal for more than a day or
two at a time, be sure that your roommates will be willing
to take responsibility for feeding your pets and plants while
you are away, and for walking or keeping an eye on any
pets that are not confined. If you can't trust any of them,
hire the kid next door.

3. If a pet or a plant becomes communal property, be sure
to schedule its care or make one person permanently
responsible for caring for it, as part of his or her regular
household duties. If one of the members of your household
is especially green-thumbed and willing to feed and water
everything, the other members of the household might want
to chip in to pay for a couple of fairly expensive plants and
the plant food as their part of the bargain.

4. If a previously approved pet turns out to be much noisier,
dirtier, or more toxic to other members of the household
than was previously expected, a family meeting should be
called to deal with the situation. Although it may cause
heartaches, the most realistic and equitable attitude seems
to be that any human being in a household is more
important than any animal and should not be forced to live
with anything that makes him or her unhappy. Of course,

there are exceptions to every situation—if only one member
of a household takes a dislike to a cat that has been a
member of the family for years before he or she arrived, the
newcomer may have to be the one to leave. And,
sometimes, airing one's grievances at a family meeting can
do much to produce some adjustments where pets are
concerned that may prevent things from getting to the "This
house is not big enough to hold both of us" stage.

Although your house is probably big enough to hold
all of you, your kitchen may not be, especially if you each
try to cook a separate meal at the same time with a host
of animals and children underfoot. Because the kitchen
is a sensitive area in any house, we've devoted all of the
next chapter to it.

CHAPTER IV

Is the Theft of *All* Your Chocolate Chip Cookies Really a Mitigating Circumstance for First-Degree Murder?

Although real estate agents have long tried to convince people that no home can be without a family room, market research and formal psychological and sociological studies have proved that the kitchen is really the heart of the home in most of the countries and cultures throughout the world.

People love to eat, and anyone who has attended a Christmas dinner knows that breaking bread together is still a potent bonding ritual. And so, although fast-food chains have burgeoned all over our planet, most of us still prefer to prepare and consume our meals in our homes—even if we're just heating up a can of soup or putting a frozen dinner in the oven. Researchers have found that this is not so much for economic reasons as it is because of the feelings of security that come from our childhood associations with Mother in the kitchen, dishing out the love and the chicken soup each day.

Even if Mother *wasn't* in the kitchen, but was out being a successful nuclear physicist or tango dancer, that was still what we learned from our first-grade readers, the novels we later enjoyed, and almost everything we

saw in the movies and on television. And this has never
changed as we've moved from "Ozzie and Harriet" and
"Father Knows Best" through "The Waltons" to whatever the hot new sit-com happens to be.

All of this indicates a basic human attitude about meal
preparation and consumption that can either create a
warm, family atmosphere in a group household or can
generate a potentially explosive situation. Unsurprisingly, researchers have also found that the kitchen is the
most dangerous place in the home—the place where the
most accidents occur. And although we're assuming that
you're smart enough to keep the poisons out of the reach
of the kids and stash a fire extinguisher near the stove,
the greatest potential danger remains—the clash of
human foibles as you come together daily at the watering
hole, and the inevitable competition for the stove, the
sink, and the pots and pans when you're trying to get off
to work in the morning or feeling pooped at the end of
the day.

Here's a case in point from our extensive collection of
communal-kitchen culinary horror stories:

Janet Blumenthal was a successful, independent
woman. She held several advanced degrees, a responsible executive position, and considered herself to be
highly liberated in every way. However, although she'd
attended self-actualization seminars and checked out
other humanistic psychological processes, she had never
examined her basic belief systems about kitchens. That
is, not until she decided to move out of her apartment
to share a large and beautiful house with three friends.

Because the four housemates were all health-con-
scious and shared many of the same tastes in food, they
agreed to share the kitchen responsibilities and take
their meals in common. Unfortunately, Janet soon made
this impossible. She insisted on ridiculously high stan-

dards of cleanliness and organization in the kitchen—
literally picked the dirt out of the grout between the
counter tiles at the end of each day—and severely chas-
tised the others if they bought something at one market
when it was on sale at another. In no time at all, her
attitude literally scared the other members of the household out of the kitchen, and Janet was left to do most of
the shopping, cooking, and cleaning up herself.

Of course, at first she didn't see it that way. All she
knew was that suddenly her roommates no longer
seemed motivated to shoulder their share of the kitchen
duties, and she resented this deeply. Fortunately, before
things got completely out of hand, her friends were able
to confront her at a family meeting in a loving and con-
structive way and help her to see what was causing their
kitchen crisis. A roommate who was a therapist explained that although Janet consciously held a liberal
and democratic set of values about most things, her unex-
amined and unconscious belief systems about how a
"good housekeeper" functioned in a kitchen were ruling
her behavior. At first, Janet resisted the idea, but after
recalling that her mother and grandmother had been fanatical housekeepers and remembering how much she'd
resented that, she was willing to admit that subcon-
sciously she had internalized their values and was now
living out the myth that any worthwhile woman kept an
immaculate and well-stocked kitchen, complete with
containers of homemade gourmet goodies in the freezer.
With the help of her roommates, she was soon able to
relax and feel good about dealing with the kitchen on a
more casual basis, and today everyone in the house is
happier for it—especially Janet.

This is only one example of how a set of housemates
can deal constructively with a problem caused by dif-
fering values. Most such problems can be solved as long

as the members of the household are open, forthright, and willing to maintain a positive attitude toward each other in spite of their differences. "A Family of Friends" will show you how to use family meetings and formal agreements to work out problems and set up equitable rules for living together. Right now, let's take a look at the problems that relate particularly to kitchen duties so we can point out the pitfalls and suggest ways of avoiding them.

TOGETHERNESS CAN BE BLISS—IF YOU PLAN PROPERLY

There are many ways to deal with the shopping, cooking, and cleaning chores, from totally communal situations where everyone does everything together, to kitchens where housemembers fend for themselves, right down to maintaining separate dishes and cooking utensils. In between are an infinite number of possibilities for creative compromise. How, then, do you decide what arrangement is right for your household? Obviously, the best way is one that creates the fewest problems; and as usual, the old Zen adage holds: *Keep it simple*. The less complicated the arrangements the better for all concerned.

We've constantly stressed the necessity of selecting housemates who are compatible with your tastes and life-style, and nowhere is this more important than when considering how to set up your kitchen. In order to decide whether you want to prepare and eat your meals together, it is important to determine whether your eating habits and patterns have enough in common to make a communal kitchen a success. Although you may have some significant differences, the value of having someone to eat with often outweighs the adjustments you may have to make, but there are cases where individual priorities, tastes, and necessities would create tensions that no household should have to endure. Accordingly, we suggest that you and your housemates each consider the following questions before you make up your minds:

Are Your Tastes in Food Compatible?

Are you a junk-food addict, into health foods and organic veggies, or somewhere in between? Are you open to trying new dishes, or are you picky and fussy about what you eat? Some of us are just not willing to be flexible about food—we want what we want when we want it, and we aren't interested in newfangled recipes or exotic adventuring. If you are like this, you probably should prepare your meals on an individual basis to avoid cramping the style of the more creative cooks in your household.

Of course, you may not be able to be flexible. If you have severe food allergies or are on a strict diet for medical or religious reasons, you will have to prepare your meals independently unless you are fortunate enough to have a roommate with the same allergies, diet, or religious beliefs.

What Are Your Eating Habits?

Are you a snacker? Or do you eat three regular meals a day? At what times do you usually take your meals? It's hard to cook in common and then eat at different times. Do you generally have breakfast? Do you eat it at home or at your desk? What about lunch? How many nights a week are you generally home for dinner? If there are big differences in these answers, then the food bills cannot be divided evenly and other arrangements will have to be worked out. Are you a compulsive eater or (perish forbid!) a binger? If so, you will probably have to contribute significantly more to the food budget than the other members of your household. Be honest about this—your roommates will know the truth anyway before long!

Can You Cook?

If not, are you willing to learn? Then, we suggest that you find housemates who are able and willing to take the time to teach you and to put up with your "interesting variations" until you've gained some skill. Of course, if you can't cook and haven't the desire and/or the time to learn, you might want to arrange to let others share the cooking while you become permanently responsible for cleaning up or doing the shopping. Many cooks will jump at such opportunities.

How Would You Prefer to Handle Shopping and Paying for the Groceries?

Some housemates decide to do their food buying and preparing communally and do all the grocery shopping together, once a week, so that everyone has a say in what is purchased and pays an equal amount right then and there. Any extras or emergency runs are recorded in the "Bible" (see Chapter III) and settled at the end of the month. Only foods for private snack stashes or guests are paid for separately.

Other housemates find it more convenient to share the food buying by taking turns doing the shopping, either as a separate weekly household duty or in conjunction with each individual's turn to cook. They generally post a shopping list where people can jot down the things they've noticed are out of stock, or need for a special dish they're going to prepare, or would just like to have in the house. Then whoever is going to the store takes along the list. In this situation, each housemate saves his or her receipts to be divided equally once a month. One person is usually chosen to handle this chore and enter the figures in the "Bible" (preferably someone with a calculator or a good head for math).

Still other groups elect to do their food buying and preparing on an individual basis, and although they may occasionally pick up a thing or two for each other, these little debts are settled privately, preferably as soon as the groceries hit the kitchen.

Whose Utensils Will You Use?

Do you have enough to stock the whole kitchen yourself, or do all your housemates plan to contribute their equipment? No matter whose stuff you use, just be sure that it is inexpensive, durable, and can be easily replaced. To avoid problems, be sure to agree beforehand that if something is broken or damaged, the culprit must pay for the replacement. We would never suggest using anyone's $200-per-place-setting china on a regular basis, even if it is open stock!

Whether you plan to share utensils or not, remember to have all your housemates mark their items clearly, either by scratching their initials into metal or wood items or by burning them in using inexpensive tools that are available at local hobby shops. Many police stations and some insurance companies allow people to borrow electric engravers to mark expensive items so they can be identified if they are ever stolen by burglars. If you also mark all your pots and ladles while you've got the tool at home, who will be the wiser? At any rate, try to get all utensils marked before they become mixed together. You may think you know what your cookie sheet looks like, but in six months, if it isn't labeled, you may find that your roommate clearly remembers that it was his or hers to begin with. If marking all that stuff is beyond the limits of your time and patience, at least make a complete list of the utensils each member of the household has contributed.

Your kitchen can also be run on a strictly individual basis, with each member using and cleaning his or her own utensils and dishes, providing that there is sufficient space to store duplicate equipment. If there is, and you want to go this route, be sure to divide the cupboards and the drawer space evenly and to mark everything anyway to avoid conflicts.

How Would You Like to Split the Cooking?

If you are going to adopt the communal approach, would you prefer to delegate one person to do the cooking for each meal? On a daily basis? For a week at a time? Or would you like to pitch in and all cook together? Although most communal kitchens have found it more convenient to assign meal preparation to one housemate at a time, it can sometimes be great fun to all pile into the kitchen and cook in tandem. We've even given dinner parties where everyone got a cutting board and chopped and minced and diced and stirred in unison. However, to prevent too many cooks from spoiling the broth, we've usually found it best to make each person responsible for a particular dish or job, such as making the salad or the sauce or dicing the veggies, and to keep out of each other's hair by not making unwarranted adjustments or indulging in uninvited sampling until the finished products are on the table.

What about Doing the Dirty Work?

When it comes to the problem of day-to-day and general cleanup, the kitchen can become the most dangerous room in the house, indeed. Whether you operate communally or on a strictly individual basis, it is vitally important that you all agree on who is to do what, for whom, and when. In many kitchens where the housemates share the cooking, the one who cooks a meal is also responsible for setting the table and cleaning up afterward. In that way, the others get to enjoy their freedom—it's almost like eating out. In other setups, one roommate cooks, another sets the table, and a third cleans up—or the two latter chores are combined so that one person is the cook and another is the "support system." In every household we've ever lived in—even in traditional nuclear families where Mommy was totally responsible for food preparation, it has been considered good manners and a family obligation for every person at the table to take part in clearing the table after the meal. This means removing the food and the dishes, helping to put the leftovers away, placing the dishes and the pots in the sink or dishwasher, and decrumbing the table. Unless you have extremely good reasons why this is unworkable in your house, we suggest that you encourage your housemates to do this as well, no matter who is ultimately responsible for washing up. It is the kind of considerate cooperation that seems to generate similar attitudes in other areas of the household.

What chores are then left for the cleanup person? Washing all the dishes and utensils, putting away the leftovers that are still in the pots, picking up any spills and scraps from the floor, and cleaning the countertop, the stovetop, and the sink. Stacking the dishes to dry is fine, if there is space. But other than that, the place should look just as it did before the preparations for the meal began.

Which brings us back to the question of *when* cleanup should occur, no matter who is responsible for doing it. Should the Cinderella of the day appear while the cooking is going on to whisk away the pots and utensils as they are no longer needed? Or should the entire mess be cleared away at once after the meal is over? Some people simply cannot rest until the dishes are done, while others like to wait until their digestive processes are well under way before they force themselves to confront the dirty kitchen. So before the grease hits the fan, you might want to agree on some cleanup deadlines (even Cinderella had to be home by midnight). It seems to us that the most flexible procedure would to be to say that the person responsible for cleaning up a communal kitchen after a specific meal must accomplish the task before the next meal is due to be prepared and that the dinner dishes have to be done before that person retires for the night.

It's up to you whether you assign the mealtime cleanups on a daily, weekly, or meal-by-meal basis, but the daily cleaning up of dishes doesn't cover everything. Over time, grease and grime have a way of accumulating between the tiles of floors and countertops and in those hidden areas behind the juicer and the microwave, under the sink, and on top of the refrigerator. The windows and walls will acquire a film of smoke and grease (not to mention fingerprints), and even if the floor is touched up after each meal, it will still need to be thoroughly swept and washed at least once a week unless you all like living in a postgraduate version of *Animal*

House. And, of course, the innards of the refrigerator, the cabinets, and the stove must be washed up every so often, too. As we've discussed in chapter III, the key is to share the work evenly and make sure it is posted on a schedule or in the "Bible." Just how you work out the shares is up to you. Here are a couple of alternatives:

The Bite-the-Bullet-and-Get-It-Over-With Approach

You each take responsibility for cleaning up the kitchen thoroughly once a week on an alternating basis and rotate the things that need to be done less frequently (such as washing the windows or the cabinets or cleaning the oven) on a monthly basis, or as they become necessary. If there are several people in your household, this brings that wonderful feeling that you've done your turn and can relax until the schedule rolls round to you again.

The Many-Hands-Make-Light-Work or Misery-Loves-Company Method

You all arrange to get together at the same time (Saturday mornings are popular) to pitch in and do the general cleanup together. This can be coordinated with cleaning up the rest of the house as well. Again, the work should be at least generally assigned, to prevent the perennial goldbricks from not doing their share, but more than one person can work at a task so that nobody has to wash all the cabinets or all the windows.

The Let-George-Do-It Approach

Hire a houseworker to come in on a weekly basis and make cleaning the kitchen thoroughly a top priority task. For more about these wonderful people, refer back to Chapter III.

A Few Tips on Individual Cooking
Arrangements

If you decide to shop and cook on an individual basis, there are a number of other things you must take into consideration. First, you will need to divide the food-storage space. What we've said earlier about dividing space in the rest of the house applies here as well: Divide the space equitably. Even if you're a gourmet cook and your housemate eats out 90% of the time, you should have equal space in the refrigerator and in the cabinets—unless you can work out a fair trade for space elsewhere.

Obviously, if you are going to cook and eat individually, each person should be responsible for returning the kitchen to order as quickly as possible. There have been households where the roommates took their meals separately, and one roommate was responsible for kitchen cleanup at the end of each day, but as far as we have seen, this rarely works out well. For one thing, some members of the household use an enormous amount of dishes and utensils, while others use relatively few and tend to clean up unconsciously as they go along. But the main problem is that it is not pleasant to come into the kitchen looking forward to making yourself a nice meal, only to find that the pans you'd like to use are full of congealed bacon grease. If you always have to wash the frying pan before you use it, you will soon be tempted to fry your roommate in it! If the table, the countertops, and the sink look like the Pied Piper and all the rats of Hamlin have paraded across them, and the stove is a cruddy mess before you begin to cook, it doesn't matter if the roommate responsible for cleaning up bounces faithfully into the kitchen after the last meal has been prepared and restores everything to pristine order. The fact is, your food would probably have been more palatable if you'd eaten at the local greasy spoon.

If your kitchen runs on an individual basis, each person should clean up his or her mess before leaving the kitchen or at least before the next person is ready to cook. No matter how big the kitchen is, or how many utensils there are—even if each person has a complete kit—it is a poor idea to allow roommates to stack their dirty dishes in an appointed place and do them at their leisure. We've seen stacks that became permanent features of the kitchen, with the offending roommates only washing the things they needed and leaving the rest to grow interesting flora and fauna forever. This is not the stuff of which happy group households are made.

Another potential problem for separate cooks is timing. Most of us like a bit of company at mealtimes, and you may be tempted to eat your separate meals at the same time. Just be sure your facilities can stand the traffic. When one or more people try to use one tiny kitchenette simultaneously, the result can be pandemonium, especially if you are sharing one inadequate set of pots and pans. The best solution is to set up a schedule based on each person's working hours and needs, so that everyone has some time alone at the stove, even if eating times overlap to some extent. Be flexible in setting up such a schedule, and be willing to change it whenever necessary, but be sure that everyone is aware of—and agrees on—the changes. This may seem like an overly formal way of dealing with the situation, but as the British explorers, who dressed for dinner in the middle of the jungle, found out a long time ago, formality can get you through some pretty hairy situations. Later, when routines have been established and everyone knows each other well, formalities such as cooking schedules can be relaxed.

Pleasant Surroundings Make for Good Digestion

It is no longer enough to simply say, "You are what you eat." Psychologists have now found that you are *how* you eat as well. Because the environment in which we dine seems to have a considerable effect on how well we digest our food, we urge you to make an effort to create a peaceful and pleasant place in which to take your meals. Even if your budget is low and you are dining off a card table in the corner of the kitchen, you can invest in some cheery curtains and a nice wipe-clean tablecloth or a set of placemats, keep unsightly clutter off the counters, and hang some baskets or other inexpensive decorations on the walls.

One advantage of group households is that children learn much more quickly to respect the rights of others than they do in the traditional nuclear family. Parents are more likely to cater to their children and to make excuses for thoughtlessness or selfish behavior than are the less emotionally involved adults who just share living space with them. The kitchen and eating area should be, and usually are, the first places where such learning experiences occur. So if there are children in your group household, please be firm about keeping the kitchen a pleasant place to be—you will be doing both yourself and everyone else a favor.

Many people have learned as children that supper time presents a terrific opportunity to air one's grievances with the whole family as a captive audience—with disastrous effects on even the most ironclad digestive systems. If we accomplish anything with this book, we would like to stop this syndrome in as many households as possible, especially in households with youngsters. The sooner the kids learn that the kitchen is a place to be well-behaved and considerate of others, the better for the digestive systems of everyone involved. To that end, whether there are children in your house or not, we strongly suggest that you make it a rule that all disagreements must be handled outside the kitchen, before or after mealtimes, even if they begin at the table.

Breaking the Sound Barriers

One problem related to kitchens and kids is that they both tend to get noisier and noisier as mealtime approaches. The combination can be deafening. If two or more adults are attempting to cook in a small kitchen, it can be exasperating (not to mention dangerous) to have little children underfoot. Or bigger children nibbling, sampling, criticizing, and demanding attention. So we suggest that parents in group households make every effort to keep the kids out of the kitchen until the meal is on the table. If you want to teach your child to cook, save the cooking lessons for quiet afternoons, when you can pay attention to one child exclusively and aren't hungry or tired yourself. Even if whining, tired children don't bother you at mealtimes, think about your housemates and make every effort to be considerate. After all, your housemates are helping you to pay the rent or the mortgage, and they provide support in other ways as well. So don't stretch your luck by pushing matters too far at mealtimes. If necessary, feed your children early, or give them a substantial snack about an hour before dinner so that they can behave like human beings instead of starved animals at the table. And don't use mealtimes to rake them over the coals for their performance at school or other misdeeds. Treat them as pleasantly as you would another adult, or better yet, as you would like to be treated by another adult. If you do this for them, they might surprise you by reciprocating.

It is also a good idea to keep pets out from under your feet while cooking and eating. You may have become deaf to the maddening yowl of your Siamese cat when you're anywhere near the refrigerator, but you can bet that your housemates won't be, no matter how much they like the dear old fellow at other times. And even though you've learned to step around the prone form of your Labrador retriever when he is sleeping on the rug in front of the sink, your housemates may find him an unnecessary inconvenience when they are rushing to prepare a quick bite between work and night school. Although you may find it cozy to chop and slice with your cat at your elbow on the kitchen counter, many people find an animal on a food-preparing surface to be revolting and unhealthy. They probably won't appreciate a pet who begs at the table either, although they might not say so for fear of offending the avid owner. If you have pets, try to be considerate of your human companions by feeding Tiger and Towzer outside or in another area of the house and keeping the kitchen free of them, especially at dinner time. Even an old raccoon can learn new tricks.

Children also need to respect property rights. Whether you're cooking together or separately, it can be a real problem when Johnny and Susie take a whole loaf of bread and feed it to the neighbor's Saint Bernard. If you were counting on that bread for your morning toast, or for sandwiches for lunch, you won't be greatly mollified to hear, "But he was hungry!" You are more likely to yell back at the baffled kids, "And so am I!"

The Case of the Mysterious Food-Snatcher

Little Max, aged six, was quite spoiled and used to having everything his own way when his parents divorced and his mother took in Ruth and Inga as housemates. The communal kitchen they set up worked out quite well until certain items began to disappear regularly from the refrigerator—especially the lunch meats that Max liked best. But there was never any proof that he was pilfering, and he denied all accusations strenuously. One morning, Ruth was brewing her morning cup of coffee and Max was eating his bowl of cereal while Inga prepared a sandwich for lunch with some particularly juicy-looking turkey breast. Ruth decided she'd make a turkey sandwich for lunch that day, too, as soon as she had washed and dressed for work. She left the kitchen and came back later only to find that there was no turkey left. She was grumbling about what a pig Inga was when Max's mother came into the room and said, "I saw Inga put back at least half a pound of meat, but when I went to take a slice for breakfast a few minutes ago, there was nothing left in the package. I thought you'd used the rest to make the fattest sandwich imaginable!"

Some quick detective work revealed that Max had been left alone in the kitchen for a few minutes and had apparently stuffed his jacket pockets full of turkey before he left for school. "I wondered why he insisted on wearing his jacket on such a warm day," his mother said, and she got into her car and made a lightning raid on her son at school. At first, Max denied any knowledge of the turkey but broke down when his teacher said she'd seen him passing out slices to his friends in the playground. That evening, everyone told Max how angry his food pilfering had made them feel. The next day, his mother took him to the store and he had to personally pay out the money he'd been saving for roller skates to renew the household's turkey supply. That seemed to cure him of snitching food from the refrigerator.

Adult food pilferers and other gluttons can be just as much of a problem in a group household. The best advice we can give here is to be open. If you are not getting your fair share of the common food supply, or if food is missing from your private stock, say something immediately, rather than letting it fester. As in most situations, the sooner an issue is dealt with, the easier it will be to handle. Here are some rules to prevent trouble before it starts:

1. Always ask permission to borrow someone's food or to use more than your share of a common food supply. If there is no one at home to ask, leave a note saying what you took and that you will replace it immediately.

2. Always replace what you have taken within twenty-four hours. If someone was counting on the food before then, go out and buy it at once, if you possibly can.

3. Never take the last piece of anything from someone else's food supply unless you have specific permission to do so.

4. When in doubt about borrowing anything, don't.

5. If you don't want anyone to borrow a particular item under any circumstances, tell everyone concerned and then label the item "Mine" so they can't possibly forget.

Of course, there is always the possibility that you may unwittingly saddle yourself with a roommate who is a compulsive eater or binger and cannot control the urge to eat everything in sight. If this happens to you, and the culprit is unwilling or unable to pay for the extra food, you may have to threaten to change roommates, unless you don't mind subsidizing such overeating indefinitely. This may seem drastic, but by being determined on this issue, you may help the person to realize that he or she has a problem that needs to be dealt with professionally.

Even if your roommate is not a foodaholic but simply eats much more than you do, you must sit down and figure out the proportionate amounts you consume and adjust the food budget accordingly, or buy separately.

Nothing Is Forever

Sometimes a food-sharing arrangement that has been working quite well for some time suddenly becomes unworkable. After all, nothing is forever. Spouses change, housemates change, and our individual needs are constantly changing, too. Take, for example, two roommates who had shared cooking responsibilities very happily for two years, with almost no problems. Then they each became seriously involved with a man. Jean's boy friend was a homebody who enjoyed family dinners and loved to spend time with her children in the evening. Ann's "significant other" was exactly the opposite. He took her out to dinner several times a week, and they spent most weekends on his boat, accompanied by her teenage son, Tom. At first, Jean's friend would arrive with a good bottle of wine or a special treat for dessert to make up for the food he ate as an impromptu member of the household, but that arrangement soon became unwieldy. Because she and Jean had been splitting the food bills down the middle, Ann was suddenly paying for far more food than she was consuming, now that she was eating so few meals at home. And for the same reason, she found it almost impossible to follow the equitable routine for cooking and cleaning up the kitchen that had worked so well until then. For a while, Tom took his mother's turn when he ate at home and she was away, but he soon began to suffer from what he called "a terminal case of dishpan hands," and this motivated him to come up with a solution. He told Ann that he felt it would be easier

on his hands and would take less time from his school-
work and other activities if he shopped and cooked for
himself when she was not at home, and she could cook
for just the two of them whenever she was. Ann agreed
and she and Jean arranged to buy and prepare food individually from then on.

But this was easier said than done. First, they had to
divide the existing supplies between them and make arrangements for separate space in the refrigerator and
cupboards. To avoid dragging out this somewhat complicated task, they set aside a Saturday and did it all at
once. In the process, they decided to continue to buy
some staples—such as flour, sugar, aluminum foil, sandwich bags, and cleaning supplies—together. Cleaning
up remained a problem for a while, because Tom tended
to snack a lot and forgot to pick up after himself, but Jean
hung some reminder notes around the kitchen. And
threatened by an enforced return to the communal dishpan, Tom soon mended his ways. As it turned out, this
resumption of individual kitchen responsibilities helped
Jean and Ann to adjust to living in separate homes once
again, when they each remarried the following year.

And now, after exploring the trials and tribulations of
togetherness in the kitchen, let's talk about what happens when togetherness gets out of hand. Our next chapter deals with the impact of lovers, guests, and other
"outsiders" on a group household.

CHAPTER V

"Good Morning, Whoever You Are!": Living with Lovers and Other Strangers

When we first thought of writing a book about group housekeeping, many of our friends and most of the publishing people we contacted assumed it was going to be an exposé of the hippie communes that flourished about twenty years ago. Now, lurid stories of dope-driven weird-os engaging in hysterical orgies certainly do sell books. But we were forced to pop the balloon by admitting that we had something much more practical in mind. Besides, most of the communes we knew of back in the sixties were a hell of a lot tamer than the parties many teenagers are now attending every weekend!

So, if you have been eagerly awaiting this chapter because you expected to be entertained by exotic accounts of orgiastic "group gropes" and sexual experimenta-tion—or by lurid tales of housemates who have stolen each other's lovers or spouses—prepare to be disap-pointed! (We were . . . a little.)

After researching this area thoroughly, we've found practically no evidence of promiscuity or communal sex in the wide variety of group households we've visited and lived in. Certainly far less than what has apparently been going on in suburban communities for years—if one can believe those rumors of "key parties" and spouse swapping among jaded couples. (Personally, we believe that most of those stories were probably spread by real estate agents and may have been responsible for the suburban housing boom of the seventies!)

Perhaps because we have focused on people who join forces for economic and social reasons, most of the members of the group households we've encountered have been independent, self-supporting professionals; business people; and single parents who have a strong sense of their own value and who tend to relate to others from a position of strength. Since these characteristics are pluses in any relationship, it stands to reason that they have helped to prevent most group households from falling into the pitfalls of overindulgence in any area—including sex.

Although problems do arise concerning the intrusion of lovers and other guests into the household routine, the issue is largely one of agreement. It really doesn't seem to matter whether housemates are casual about overnight lovers, live-in lovers, or long-term guests—or are militantly against them—as long as everyone in the house feels the same way. And when it comes to violent antipathy concerning nocturnal visits, we've found more people reacting to the stress it places on space and privacy than resisting for reasons of morality. Even in housefuls of swinging singles—who are now so numerous they have earned the generic title "swingles"—most roommates were seriously concerned with setting up a structure that would allow them to socialize without intruding on one another's privacy and need for peace and quiet.

At a recent workshop on group living sponsored by the Share-A-Home agency, which focused on group living situations that incorporate elderly or handicapped people into nuclear or single-parent families, the attendees were divided into groups of six to simulate household meetings. When asked to discuss one of several suggested topics, one group chose "Overnight Guests: Sexual and Nonsexual." Of the six people in this rather conservatively oriented group, one adamantly opposed allowing guests in the house for sexual purposes; another was not concerned about visitors of the opposite sex but would not countenance a housemate having a homosexual affair; and the rest were quite willing to play the matter by ear, but did not want any housemate to have guests for more than three consecutive days without prior agreement from the other household members. They also wanted a stipulation that any housemate who entertained guests must contribute extra money for food and other household expenses.

Most group households usually wind up with similar general guidelines regarding guests, if their members are sensitive to each other's needs. And those who aren't generally find themselves seeking other housemates before long!

Since it is so important that all members of a household agree on these issues, we suggest that you take another look at the questions in Chapter II that address this area and be sure that your prospective housemates can reach agreement, or at least a friendly compromise, that you all can live with before you move in together.

Of course, even if housemates are in basic agreement about houseguests and lovers, problems will still arise, but before you run screaming for the nearest residential hotel, we're going to devote the rest of this chapter to ways to prevent them from occurring, and the things to do when they come up anyway. Just to keep things in perspective, we'll explore some of the major disaster areas in terms of "real-life stories with happy endings."

One of the chief objections to inviting lovers to stay over is the fear of the effect this might have on the children in the household. Although our first story deals with a mother and her child, the question often comes up when single housemates bring lovers into houses where other people's children reside. The issue is the same in either case, and the adults in the house usually need more reassurance than the youngsters do. Kids tend to take most things in stride, and can react to the most bizarre situations with sophisticated equanimity—providing that the feelings that lie behind them are loving and positive. Any child that has lived through the acrimonious nocturnal debates of parents that are on the verge of divorce can certainly handle the presence of someone loving and respectful in a single parent's bedroom—or anyone else's for that matter. The real question seems to be whether the parent objects to the idea of sex between unmarried adults and does not want to expose his or her children to any other loving physical relationships besides marriage. As promised, our first story asks the following poignant question:

Can a Mother Find Love and Sexual Fulfillment with a Teenage Kid in the Next Room?

After her divorce, Jena Trilling and her teenage daughter Lindsey rented a house with two other women. Although each of them had a bedroom of her own, Jena and Lindsey shared one bathroom, and the only way for Lindsey to get to it was through her mother's room. At first, this didn't inconvenience her in any way. Then circumstances began to change.

The other women in the house had men friends who occasionally spent the night with them, and this did not bother Jena at all. She felt that Lindsey needed to know that love was an essential part of living and that physical affection could be expressed without shame or the need for dependent relationships. She might have objected to a continuing stream of strange men running through the house, but neither of her roommates was promiscuous, and everyone in the household had generally met and accepted a particular man long before he was invited to spend the night.

However, several months after she and her daughter had moved into the household, Jena noticed that she was not living up to her own liberal beliefs. She only stayed out overnight on the weekends that Lindsey went to visit her father, and she never brought anyone home with her at all. When she found herself refusing to allow a man she especially liked and desired to spend the night because Lindsey might come home unexpectedly, Jena realized that the "fifties' morality" she thought she'd left far behind was reasserting itself. It wasn't that she was ashamed of having a sex life—she and Lindsey had talked about it and agreed that this was a normal part of living. She wanted her daughter to know that even if a marriage did not work out, a person could pick up the pieces and find love and happiness again. But the thought of her daughter coming through her bedroom and finding her in bed with a lover was something Jena wasn't sure she could handle.

Once she realized this, Jena knew that although the problem was clearly the result of her own "stuff," sooner or later she would start to resent Lindsey for unwittingly putting a cramp in her love life. Since she didn't want to trade the master bedroom and bath for Lindsey's smaller room, she decided to have another talk with her daughter about the situation.

Lindsey listened attentively while her mother explained that she had been dating a man for some time and was beginning to want something more than hugs and kisses from him. "Would you be upset if I asked him to sleep over some night?" Jena asked with some trepidation.

"Oh, no! Not at all! I was beginning to be afraid that nobody loved you!" exclaimed Lindsey, giving her mom a hug.

"But remember, you will have to come through my room on the way to the bathroom," Jena reminded her.

"No problem, I'll just knock before I come in so you can get covered up," her child responded unconcernedly.

Jena felt quite reassured, and a few nights later asked her friend to stay over. She was still a bit uneasy, however, when she heard Lindsey's alarm clock go off the next morning. When she heard a soft knock on the door, she mumbled, "Come in," and lay feigning sleep as Lindsey casually walked through the room and into the bathroom. Jena relaxed a bit as she heard the usual sounds of Lindsey washing her face and brushing her teeth, followed by her daughter's footsteps back across the room. Perhaps Lindsey was unaware that there were two forms, instead of one, under the covers. The footsteps paused midway, however, and Jena knew her daughter had realized that her mother was not alone in bed. After what seemed like an interminable pause, the bomb dropped. Lindsey cleared her throat and cheerfully greeted the visitor with devastating politeness: "Good morning . . . whoever you are!"

Although the introductions that followed were accomplished quite amiably, Jena had some difficulty afterward convincing her friend that Lindsey's comment did *not* mean that he was one of an endless string of lovers—in fact, that quite the reverse was true. It did teach her a lesson, however: From that day forward she made sure that her daughter met the men she dated, or at least knew their names, and she always made sure to tell Lindsey if she thought she might bring someone home with her for the night.

Although this incident involved a mother and daughter, it points up something that should be a standard operating procedure in any group household. Awkward things can happen when unsuspecting housemates awake to confront a stranger in the hall or the bathroom. No matter how liberally we may have been raised, it is just plain embarrassing to stumble into a naked stranger in the shower. Who knows what we may say or do under such circumstances? Therefore, we suggest that you make the following agreement:

Always try to introduce the special people in your life to your roommates, or at least let them know in advance if you might be bringing your date home for the night.

(If you strike out, they probably won't tease you. These things happen to everybody.)

TOO LONG IS MORE THAN ENOUGH

More frequently, it is not the nature of the guest, but the *duration of the stay* that creates conflict. Some people just love to entertain and consider prolonged visits from friends and relatives to be mini-vacations. Others resent the intrusion, especially if the intruders are strangers to them. Most group households are put together by people who are willing to sacrifice some space and privacy in order to live more economically. Since long-term guests can seriously strain the structures of the most harmonious traditional households, you can imagine their impact on a family of strangers.

We recently came across a poignant letter in a popular advice column that makes the point clearly. The writer complained that although he and his girl friend had taken a large apartment because they liked out-of-town guests, her parents had been staying with them for a week or two out of every month for the past half year. To make matters worse, they insisted on camping out on the sofa in the living room because they disliked the bed in the guest room. Since the writer had no desire to give up either his apartment, his relationship, or his privacy, he was at an impasse. To our delight, the columnist responded that he had a right to insist that his girl friend's parents use the guest room—even if they had to buy another bed. She also urged him to seek an agreement limiting the frequency and duration of any guest's visit—and suggested that one weekend per month would be plenty!

Just what agreement you reach will depend on the size and nature of your household and the personal preferences of your housemates. Because we live in a resort area, we both have had more than our share of out-of-town guests each year and have responded to them in our own individual ways. While Deanna established a rule that nobody could stay more than a week in her household, Teona happily entertained one guest for three months. Again, it's a matter of taste and agreement. By drawing guidelines that apply to everybody, you can assure yourself that no would-be visitor will take it personally when you limit a visit to a specific period of time. Just shrug and say, "Sorry, but it's the house rules."

Here are some typical agreements we've encountered in group households. You can see that they run the gamut from extreme rigidity to total anarchy. They have all worked quite well—as long as everyone felt fine about abiding by them:

1. No guest may be invited to eat or sleep in the house unless all housemates are notified in advance and agree to the visit.

2. Guests may be invited to share meals anytime as long as the host pays for or provides the food.

3. Any guest may sleep over as long as the host informs all housemates in advance that someone is coming. If the visit is too spontaneous to notify housemates without waking them, a note indicating that there is an overnight guest in the house should be posted on the kitchen bulletin board to avoid embarrassing surprises.

4. Housemates are free to have overnight guests at any time as long as they sleep in the housemate's room. Visits requiring the use of the living room sofa bed (or guest room) must have prior approval of housemates before guests are invited to use them.

5. No guest may stay more than one night without prior approval.

6. No guest may stay more than three nights without prior approval.

7. No guest may stay more than one week under any circumstances.

8. Any guest is fine for any length of time, without approval, providing the host is responsible for the cost of extra food and utilities consumed by the guest.

In addition to giving your housemates advance notice of overnight guests—and introducing them if possible—

127

it is also important to see to it that your guests are aware of any household rules and practices they might unwittingly run up against. For example, if you fail to inform a guest that all housemembers have agreed to keep their basic bathroom ritual under fifteen minutes on workday mornings so that everyone can get out of the house on time, you can hardly blame the poor soul when a riot ensues as he or she languishes in the tub reading the morning news. And guess who will have to take the guff (and probably pay the bill) when the hood ornament on your guest's classic roadster is torn off by the automatic garage door because you forgot to mention that no one is supposed to park in the driveway? Which brings us to the delicate subject of—

The Care and Feeding of Guests in a Group Household

We're sure you'll be intensely thrilled to discover that this entire question can be handled with elegant simplicity if you always follow our Golden Rule for hospitality:

> **Each individual host or hostess is ultimately responsible for the care, feeding, and behavior of his or her guests.**

How does this work out in practical terms?

You can each make your own decisions about whether or not to require your guests to help with the cleanup at mealtimes and to clean up after their own snacks; but please remember, if they fail to do it, you must do it for them. Not only that, if the members of your household buy their food separately, you must see to it that your guests know this and do not poach on someone else's supplies. If you've forgotten to tell a guest that the food on the right half of the refrigerator belongs to your roommate, you may awaken to find yourself accused of braunschweiger theft because he or she made a midnight snack while you snored away in innocent bliss.

If the members of your household buy food communally, be sure to contribute extra money to cover the expense of feeding your guests while they are in the house. It may be acceptable to occasionally ask roommates who are doing the cooking if they will throw an extra chop or two in the pot for your visitors, but if your guests are staying for more than one meal, be willing to take extra turns at the cooking and cleanup without waiting to be asked, or be prepared to cook for your guests yourself.

And, of course, if you invite people over who tend to get sloppily drunk, practice the tuba interminably, or make obscene advances to your roommates, you will have to be responsible for keeping them in line or showing them the door. Remember, for a group household to succeed you must really believe that keeping your roommates happy is far more vital to your own happiness than indulging any guest.

And that includes the ability to be flexible. A roommate who is usually quite happy to put up with houseguests under normal circumstances might justifiably want a moratorium on entertaining while he or she is struggling with final exams, illness, or a professional high-pressure period. So even if you've all agreed that a three-day stay is just fine, it's always a good idea to check with your housemates before you invite someone to stay at your home for *any* period of time. This kind of consideration will more than pay off in good feelings all around where you and your guests are concerned.

WHO WOULD HAVE THOUGHT WE'D EVER
SETTLE DOWN?

Flexibility also counts when circumstances change and it is time to consider changing the rules on a permanent basis. What may have suited your household perfectly at one time may not necessarily work well several months later. For example, Larry, Joe, and Harvey met at a singles bar right after each of them had gone through a divorce. Over beers each confided that he had been a pretty steady sort of a fellow throughout his marriage and was looking for a chance to enjoy the kind of action he'd only dreamed about while reading men's magazines. Delighted to find themselves in the company of other would-be playboys, the three men agreed to rent a three-bedroom house and turn it into a "party-pad" where they could live out their fantasies.

The fun went on for months, with all-night poker games, parties every weekend, and a satisfactory stream of ladies who stayed for varying periods of time. If guests were too drunk to drive home, nobody minded if they crashed in the living room when the party was over. Everyone agreed that Larry, Joe, and Harvey were truly "three wild and crazy guys!"

Unfortunately, after a while our three heroes realized that some people were taking advantage of the situation to freeload for days. The house always seemed to have a couple of "friends" who had come for the party and stayed for the weekend—or the week. And very few of them put their hands in their pockets to contribute toward the food and drink they consumed.

Harvey was the first one to object. His high alimony and child support had him on a relatively tight budget, and he couldn't afford to play host to the world. He called a household meeting to set up some rules regarding guests and suggested that they establish a kitty and insist that people who stayed for more than one night ante up some money for food and other expenses. The house-mates agreed to post a notice that uninvited overnight guests would be expected to pay $6 per day and that this figure would go up to $10 per day if a guest stayed more than a week. The notice also stated that guests would be expected to wash their own dishes, make their own beds, and clean up the bathroom after themselves. Unsurprisingly, the number of visiting moochers soon dropped dramatically.

Once quiet had replaced chaos, Larry, Joe, and Harvey began to find that they were enjoying the privacy of their living room at night. They began to spend time together, reading and listening to music, watching television, and engaging in quiet conversation. They had moved out of their party phase and had adjusted their household rules accordingly.

Of course, your household might find itself moving in the opposite direction, toward more liberal rules, once your housemates discover that they have developed enough trust in, and respect for, one another to feel secure that their privacy won't be impinged upon seriously and that their roommates' discretion and good taste can be relied upon to keep undesirables away from the house.

THINGS THAT GO *BUMP* IN THE NIGHT

There are some circumstances, however, when the presence of an overnight guest can cause problems that are unanticipated and undetected by the host or hostess. For instance, aside from the classic "nude man in the shower" situation mentioned above, there is the nearly

universally known situation that arises from "things that
go *bump* in the night." This can take the form of the
inhuman torture a friend of ours went through one night
as he lay in bed listening to an unknown man in the room
above him going through his bedtime routines. The ceil-
ing was thin and the floor squeaked, and our friend got
caught up in translating the sounds he heard into actions.
He heard the silk rustle as the man removed his tie. He
heard the bedclothes being turned down. He followed
the man across the room as he went to hang his clothes
in the closet. The bedsprings sang out as the man sat
down to remove his shoes. *Bump*! One shoe landed on
the floor . . . and the second *bump* never came! Our
friend swears he was up half the night waiting for the
other shoe to drop.

Households that allow sleep-over lovers will almost
inevitably run into a problem with nighttime noise that
is even more discombobulating to housemates in adja-
cent rooms. And if you are not prepared to handle this
awkward situation with tact, goodwill, and understanding, you should probably opt for a different living arrangement. If your housemate's bed suddenly develops
a rhythmic squeak in the middle of the night, or the sighs
and moans of lovemaking disturb your slumber, think of
how you would feel if you were interrupted at such a
time before you pound on the wall. Just plug your ears
with cotton and wait until morning. Then, talk to your
housemate *in private*. Noisy lovers usually are blissfully
unaware that their ecstasy is being broadcast through the
walls and floorboards. Once you've brought the fact to
their attention, there is usually a quick application of oil
to the noisy bed and considerable muffling on the part
of moaners and groaners. If you are cheerfully informed
that they don't care if the world hears their passion, or
if the noise persists, then do not hesitate to confront your

housemate again and suggest that a motel might be a better place for further assignations if they do not wish to correct the problems at home.

We've found these measures to be unnecessary in most households. Not only are most people sensitive to the needs of those they choose to live with, but perhaps more importantly, few people are eager to provide blow-by-blow coverage of their sex lives to those not actively involved. We all value privacy and most of us have been taught to be very discreet about matters of the heart—and even more so about matters involving other parts of our anatomies!

LIVE-IN LOVERS: ARE THEY GUESTS—OR PESTS?

No matter how dutiful a roommate is about all of the above, a whole new set of problems can come up when he or she falls madly (or sanely, as the case may be) in love. Lovers naturally want to spend as much time together as possible, and this usually means that even if they maintain separate residences, they usually wind up together, in his or her abode. If the place they choose to spend most of their time in happens to be a group household, pressures and tensions can increase because of the continual presence of an extra person who is not a "real" member of the group. And this will double and triple if other housemates follow suit and settle down with lovers of their own. A bathroom that was adequate for three roommates is going to have a hard time accommodating six.

One of the most ticklish aspects of such situations is that you can suddenly find yourself living intimately with people you didn't choose to live with, with the onus of breaking up a love match if you complain. You can easily feel trapped into a "like it or leave it" situation, and maybe even feel that the lovers would like you to leave, because you're cramping their style.

Because it calls for a good deal of timing and tact, the solution to this problem is one of the most difficult your group household may ever have to face. But it's worth tackling—if you can bring it off. When you see that a housemate's lover has become an unofficial member of the household, it is time to invite your housemate to use a family meeting to formalize the situation in some way. Your housemate may be a bit touchy about this, for fear that his or her lover might feel pressured into a permanent relationship when it was so easy to live together unofficially without commitments. This, however, is not your problem. Gently point out that you are not pushing them into a permanent relationship, you simply want the relationship that *you* have with your housemate's lover to be one you can all feel comfortable with. By making this clear, you and your other housemates can be free to choose to take on the new person as an official member of the household (with all the obligations and duties that go with it), to reject the idea and allow the lovers to find more congenial surroundings, or to come up with one of the almost infinite number of alternatives that lie between these two extremes.

Whether the lovers stay on or leave to be replaced by a new housemate, your group household is going to find itself going through a period of transition. Rules and behavior patterns that fit one situation inevitably need to be changed when new people enter the scene, especially if it means adding an extra member to the household, and the lovers are going to have to adjust to their new status as well. It is hard enough to go through the first months of setting up housekeeping with a lover without having to play the whole drama out with a set of housemates as an audience. And when the housemates are having to adjust to the new status quo as well, it can be upsetting and disorienting for everyone involved, even when everyone is heartily in favor of the new arrangements. If the lovers choose to leave and a new roommate arrives, he or she is going to have to handle the awkwardness of being "the new kid" for the first couple of weeks.

WELCOMING A NEW ADDITION TO YOUR HOUSEHOLD

The best way to handle transitional periods is to keep the communication flowing and give yourself and others as much emotional support as possible. Don't expect to muddle through gallantly. Instead, take the attitude that things are probably going to be fairly hairy at first and try to join together to face whatever comes up with good humor and consideration.

Try to be especially sensitive to those unspoken messages and to encourage any roommates who seem to be uneasy or unhappy to deal openly with their feelings at family meetings. Often, the new person wants desperately to put his or her best foot forward and will try to avoid any issue that could cause a ripple. New housemates may agree to things they are not really happy about and become resentful afterward. If you are all committed to being open about your fears and concerns, negative emotions will not have a chance to explode with volcanic force because they've been repressed. So the rule should be:

> **The most unacceptable thing a roommate can say is to say nothing at all about a situation that is not to his or her liking.**

It is also especially important at these times to share your appreciation, enthusiasm, and gratitude for the good things you have created together, and to make an extra effort to help the members of your household feel like a family of friends.

DEALING WITH THE "ODD MAN OUT" SYNDROME

Sometimes a household takes on a triangular configuration, with one or two pairs of lovers in residence plus an original roommate who is still unattached. As one woman who found herself in this situation commented: "I know it's not their fault, but I constantly feel like a 'leftover.' Like someone's spinster aunt. Everyone else is so blissfully in love, and I stay home on weekend evenings and play chess with my roommate's teenage daughter—unless she has a date, too. I know that everyone really wants me to stay, and I hate the prospect of having to start up again in another group house where I'll probably have to go through being the new one in the group, but I'm considering leaving." This woman did leave. To everyone's surprise, she chose to share an apartment in town with a man with whom she had worked for some time. "We're just friends," she explained, "and that is what we'll always be. But we have learned to get along together in the office, and we have lots of tastes in common. I think we'll be able to help each other meet new people, too. It sure feels better than being the 'odd man out!'"

To her delight, her relationships with her former roommates have remained close. They party together, meet for lunch, and she even gets together with her former roommate's daughter for a game of chess "for old times' sake." "Now I have the best of both worlds," she claims.

"The friendship and support is still there—and my social life has picked up considerably."

Although there were no wild scenes in it, we hope this chapter has been a challenging experience for you after all. By confronting one of the most delicate aspects of group living, you will be better prepared to find roommates and form agreements that will help your household deal with any issues that may arise when lovers and other strangers appear on your doorstep or in your beds. Of course, the entire problem of additions to your household—whether they be guests, lovers, or new roommates—is largely one of privacy. We get to that in the next chapter.

CHAPTER VI

"All I Want Is a Little Peace and Quiet!"

Perhaps you would be all in favor of living with other people if it were not for one recurring nightmare: You come home from work at the end of a long, hot, pressured day looking forward to pouring yourself a nice cold beer, taking a leisurely cool soak in the tub, and settling yourself down in your favorite chair to read the paper and dream away the evening, while soft music and a gentle air conditioner soothe away your cares. Instead, you find the house filled with people. The living room and the kitchen are overflowing with your roommates and their friends. Hard rock is blasting from the stereo. All the beer in the house has been drained by moochers. The air conditioner has failed to cope with the constant traffic in and out of the house. Your brief stay in the bathroom is interrupted repeatedly by importunate beer drinkers who can't wait. You retreat to your room only to find that your bed is occupied by some unknown couple, and they are clearly too involved with each other to be interrupted. You are too tired to go anywhere, and there is literally no place to go.

This is not a fantasy. We have encountered similar scenes in a number of group households—most of them short-lived. It is sometimes hard for the wills and whims of several people to be accommodated within the confines of one small space. But if too many housemates find themselves at odds with the general atmosphere on too many occasions—and have no sanctuary to retreat to— there will be a For Rent sign hanging in the window before long.

Since it is almost inconceivable that you and your housemates will all want to sleep, or party, or play music at precisely the same time, *all the time*, how can your household provide a space for everyone to do his or her thing simultaneously? Obviously, it can't always do that, but with a bit of planning, consideration, and communication, you can probably manage to live together harmoniously—on most occasions.

Exploring The Borders Of Togetherness

Basically, privacy comes in three flavors: It can be protection from being seen, from being heard, or from being intruded upon. A successful group household must provide the room and opportunity for its inhabitants to find a "safe space" in which to retreat from the general environment—and that space must be available whenever it is needed.

Being seen is probably the most obvious aspect of this issue. Few people want to use the toilet or the tub in front of anyone who just happens to come in. We may be willing to sit around in our undies with our roommates—or to strip completely and share a hot tub with friends—but we want to do it only when it suits us, and not have to live out our lives in full view of the world. Therefore, any group household should have bathroom and bedroom doors that lock from the inside. And people who intend to enter should knock first, *every time*!

If your dwelling is seriously deficient in the bathroom area, and it's either a matter of sharing the bathroom at the same time or being late for work, it would be wise to invest in a cheap shower curtain or use a secondhand screen (one of those three-paneled folding jobs will do) or a bamboo blind to provide at least the illusion of privacy for those using the tub or the john.

"ALL I WANT IS A ROOM SOMEWHERE . . ."

As we've mentioned before, we also strongly urge that—with the possible exception of young children and couples—every member of the household should have his or her own room. (To be perfectly frank, we feel that kids and couples would probably benefit from having individual rooms, too, but often the exigencies of money and space give them no choice.) True, there are many group apartments, especially those occupied by students, that manage to cram two or three people into a bedroom and have housemates that sleep on the couch as well. There have even been situations in hospitals and prisons where hundreds of people have occupied the same living space. These are impressive testimonies to the adaptability of human beings, but we are aiming at happiness and harmony here. You are probably reading this book because you want to improve the quality of your life—not set an endurance record. So although it may look wonderful on paper to add that extra person to that nice, large master bedroom—be warned that the extra rent money you gain will probably not repay you for the friction and problems that living in each other's laps will cause.

Not only do individual bedrooms provide freedom from the prying eyes of others, they also offer a place to stow your possessions securely. If your precious jazz records reside in the living room, they will hardly remain as pristinely clean and in order as they will in your own room. The same goes for your books, photos, mementos, and other stuff. And what about those personal letters, school and business papers, and bank statements? Do you really want them open to everyone in the house? There is a lot more to having your own room than just having a place to entertain an overnight guest.

In some households, people also have locks on the *outside* of their bedroom doors, and they lock them whenever they leave the house. If this security feels right to you, by all means do it. If not, at least make it a rule that housemates keep out of each other's rooms and desks—and do not borrow each other's belongings—unless they have permission.

Yours, Mine, and . . . Mine

When Janice and Bernice moved in together, they seemed to be perfectly suited to one another. Although Janice came from a relatively poor background, while Bernice had always had everything she wanted, their education, interests and personalities were very compatible. Bernice was generous to a fault. She would buy a new dress, wear it once, and thrust it upon Janice in a burst of generosity. Unfortunately, she assumed that everyone was as unconcerned about material things as she was. Because Janice had always had to pinch pennies, she carefully considered every purchase before she made it. If she bought an article of clothing, she knew it had to last for a long time. Therefore, she resented Bernice's assumption that because her clothes meant nothing to her, Janice would feel the same way about her meager wardrobe. Janice seethed for a week when Bernice borrowed her new silk blouse and returned it with ketchup on it. The whole thing came to a head on New Year's Eve when Janice went to her closet to get the gorgeous and expensive dress she'd bought for the occasion, only to find it missing.

"Have you seen my new gown?" she asked Bernice.

"Oh, yeah, I borrowed it last weekend while you were away," Bernice answered unconcernedly. "Why, did you want it?"

Janice controlled her temper with difficulty. "Yes, I did want it. That is why I saved my money for weeks to buy it to wear tonight. Where is it?"

Bernice looked uncomfortable. "Well, I got this teeny stain on it and I knew you hate stains so I sent it to the cleaners . . . and I forgot to pick it up!"

Although Bernice offered Janice any gown she wanted from her extensive collection, the partnership was never quite the same after that. Bernice finally got the point after Janice got a lock for her bedroom door, and they parted a few months later when Bernice tried to borrow Janice's boyfriend!

"But I Like Early Orange-Crate!"

Your own room also offers a chance for you to create your own mini-environment. The rest of the house may be furnished in Danish Modern, but you can luxuriate in Thrift-Store Victorian or Unremitting Chaos if you prefer—once you enter your own room. Here, your favorite chair is always waiting, your tape deck can murmur exotic music for your ears alone, and you can pick your toenails if you want to.

APPRECIATING THE SOUND OF SILENCE

So much for the visual. Let's take a look at the auditory aspects of privacy for a moment. After successfully protesting air and water pollution, the environmentalists have come up with the concept of noise pollution, and they maintain that it can be as destructive to life as toxic wastes. We agree with them wholeheartedly—having had an idyllic stay in the remote desert torn asunder by the roar of dirt bikes that persisted like furious mosquitoes for hours!

Dr. Steven Halpern, a noted composer and musician, is the author of *Tuning the Human Instrument*. As an authority on the effects of sound on the human body, he has found that we listen to sounds, not just with our ears, but on the cellular level—and certain types of music and noise can have a destructive effect on our mental and physical health. He has demonstrated this by simply tapping on a table and showing that the muscles of his subjects become stronger or weaker as he varies the beat!

In *The Secret Life of Plants*, research is described in which plants were exposed to various kinds of music, with astonishing results. The plants that were placed in greenhouses in which speakers played classical music grew toward the speakers and wrapped themselves around them. These plants flourished, while similar plants who were confined with speakers that played loud, hard rock music withered and crowded as far from the speakers as they could get. So if a particular kind of music drives you batty, it may not simply be a matter of personal taste.

Obviously, the members of any group household must agree to respect the musical tastes of their housemates— either by confining objectionable music to their own rooms, or by using earphones when others aren't in the mood to hear it. The same goes for any kind of noise— loud conversations, screaming and yelling at the children in the household, using power tools, and as we noted in the last chapter, love sounds, too.

But what if everyone in the household just loves to hear The Who destroy their instruments—except Harry? And what if Henrietta is so plagued by headaches that even the slightest murmur above a whisper drives her nuts? You guessed it: Harry will be happier living with another Montovani fan, and Henrietta probably will be happier living alone. Again, the sounds in your house must be a matter of consensus, or the friction just won't be worth it for anyone. At a recent group-living workshop, participants were asked to indicate what conditions they would refuse to tolerate. Although several people responded to such items as young children, roommates of the opposite sex, etc., when loud noises were mentioned, every hand in the house went up.

How Much Privacy Is Enough For You?

For some of us, any intrusion is more than an invasion of privacy, it's a threat to our livelihood as well. Many people who work at home (and the authors have found themselves in this position) virtually barricade themselves behind closed doors and answering machines to avoid interruptions that can annihilate an hour's concentration. Such people should definitely look for housemates that are away for long periods during each day, and for rooms that are somewhat separate from the rest of the house, even if they end up working in a converted pantry, garage, or attic. If you can't come up with a housemate who is gone from 8 A.M. to 6 P.M. each weekday, then try to find someone who also works at home and who needs as much silence and privacy as you do. Teona wrote parts of this book in a house that she shared with a dressmaker who worked out of a converted playroom on the other side of the building. Deanna works out of a room at the top of her house, leaving the lower floor to her son and her housemate. Not only do the other members of the household respect her need for privacy and quiet—they often run interference for her when people drop in during working hours.

DEFENDING YOUR TURF

Of course, there is no way to create what Hemingway called "a clean, well-lighted place" for yourself if you are unwilling or unable to voice your needs and stand up for your territorial rights if necessary. Again, the good old family meeting is the place to air grievances and to forewarn housemates of stressful periods (like final exams) when you will need an extra measure of peace and quiet. However, if you find yourself right in the middle of a situation that is distasteful, you will have to speak out, right on the spot, and tell the offenders that they must knock first, stop practicing the drums, stop reading your mail, or prevent their pet from using your bedspread as a litter box. At the same time, you must also be ready and able to respond to the objections of your housemates with the same willingness to change your behavior in order to alleviate their discomfort. We all tend to get on each other's nerves at times, and the best way to survive in a group household is to realize that a happy roommate is a joy to live with and a pearl beyond price—and to feel that your housemates want you to be happy, too. If there is someone in your group household who habitually is inconsiderate, belligerent, or hard to get along with, it is probably best for all concerned if that member is asked to find more congenial surroundings.

And now, for those of us who have kids of our own, or who are eager (or adamantly opposed) to living with other people's offspring, let's turn our attention to the younger members of group households and see how they fit into the picture.

CHAPTER VII

"She's Not My Sister, We Just Live Together": Living with Your Own Kids or with Other People's Children

Living with your own kids can be difficult; living with someone else's can be even worse. But believe it or not, it can also be a wonderful experience for all concerned. Some of you are probably saying, "What would I want to live with kids for? Who needs the noise, let alone the responsibility?" And those of you who already have children may be thinking, "No way would I want to have to deal with *more* kids than I already have!"

Well, hang in there. Other people's children can bring new and rewarding dimensions to your life. And learning to live with people of *any* age can help your own children become more aware, more thoughtful, more flexible and much more able to handle a lifetime of dealing with others. Not only that, odd as it may seem, the burdens of single parenting can actually be *relieved* by sharing your living space with still more children, provided that another parent is part of the deal.

Group housekeeping family-style offers an infinite variety of options to suit an individual's age, personality, family size, and life-style. We're going to discuss some of the most popular arrangements, and you will probably be able to come up with others that are even more suitable to your own needs. We'll also get into some of the problems that can arise when you live with someone else's children, and we'll suggest some time-tested ways to avoid or deal with these problems (and the kids).

Let's begin by looking at the issue from the kids' point of view. There are special considerations when it comes to choosing the proper housemates where children are concerned. For instance:

IS IT REALLY FUN TO PLAY TWINS?

Most parents quite naturally think of looking for housemates with children who are around the same age as their own, so the kids can play together and the parents can commiserate with one another. Oddly enough, while this idea may have its good points, and may even work well in some cases, all too often it results in utter bedlam. As single parents who have lived through several kinds of arrangements, we have learned that it is better to look for *neighbors* with children the same age as your own, and to find *housemates* with significantly older or younger children or with no children at all.

We have found, to our surprise, that the most successful group housekeeping situations we've encountered often consist of people who are quite different from one another in certain ways. When we thought about it, this made good sense, especially with regard to children. Although there are exceptions to every rule, kids generally get tired of being with their peers for long periods of time. They see enough kids their own age at school and at play, and the competition is usually pretty keen. When they come home, they're ready for something different. If they're faced with more kids their own age, the stage is ripe for all kinds of rivalry, hostility, and competition for the center of attention. If a child feels that he or she is already getting the skimpy end of a hard-working parent's attention, introducing rivals the same age into the household is practically an invitation to murder. In fact, *any other youngster* may be too much, unless it is an infant the child can nurture and feel superior to, or one who is willing and able to be a loving "big brother" or "big sister." Even then there probably will be occasional jealousies and tensions to deal with, but they usually prove to be valuable growth experiences in the long run. (At least that's what we keep telling ourselves!)

"Time on My Hands": Teenagers and Senior Citizens

These days, the teenage children of working parents often spend their after-school hours watching TV or lounging around video arcades, pumping their money and energy into electronic games and feeling bored, useless, and without direction. Meanwhile, their parents are at work, knowing they really *should* be doing something to occupy their children's time more constructively, but just not having the time nor the energy to be with them more than they are.

Group living situations can provide budding young adults with a fuller life and can offer opportunities that will help them to deal more effectively with the real world beyond home and school. Living with people of different ages, backgrounds and interests can extend their circle of acquaintances beyond their parents and peers. It can give them a sense of the wide variety of choices available to them in life by exposing them to people who lead their lives differently. For example, by living with a senior citizen, teenagers can gain a sense of the richness of experience that comes with advancing years. This is something they would never develop during short, infrequent visits with grandparents who live in another city or state. By being exposed to the wisdom of a healthy senior citizen, they will not only have access to some good advice, but they will avoid the dehumanizing view of old age that has ruined the final years of many people in this country.

And kids aren't the only ones who benefit from being around oldsters. As we have gotten older ourselves, it has been a wonderful thing to learn from contact with vigorous seniors that old age can be a healthy, active, and fulfilling time of life. Several studies have recently shown that older people are healthier and happier when in daily contact with children, especially babies. We have also found that teenagers and senior citizens actually have a lot in common. Both groups often feel bored and useless in a society where you need to be over twenty-one and under sixty-five to get most of the good jobs.

The case of Chip Wilcox and Harold Gunderson is an excellent example of how a teenager and a senior citizen can enrich each other's lives:

When sixteen-year-old Chip became too difficult for his mother to handle, she sent him to live with his father. Chip had gotten heavily into drugs and was getting poor grades at school because he'd been cutting most of his classes to hang around the neighborhood video arcade. He had also totaled two cars—one before he was legally old enough to drive. In addition, he was generally rude and foul-mouthed to just about everyone.

Chip's father, Robert, was even less of a success in dealing with Chip than his mother had been. Although he laid down the law with impressive authority, he simply was not home enough to enforce his demands. The person who was home was Harold Gunderson, Robert's housemate.

When Robert had bought a big old house after his divorce, he had intended to get a roommate of his own age or younger—perhaps, he told his friends, even a "swinging chick or two." But when Harold, a retired carpenter, had answered Robert's ad, he had liked the old man instantly, because he reminded him of his own grandfather, who had also been a carpenter. When Harold offered to help him fix up the house, Robert had abandoned his plans for a playboy's pad and Harold happily moved in.

At first, Chip referred to Harold as "that old geezer" and was as rude as he could be to him. Harold wisely said nothing but went calmly about his work as though he hadn't heard a word. At that time, Harold was busy restoring the lovely maple paneling in the living room.

As Chip lounged around the house watching TV, he gradually became curious about what Harold was doing. "Why do you whistle all the time?" he asked one day.

The old man stopped and thought for a moment. It was probably the first time in months, perhaps years, that an adult had appeared to give serious consideration to one of Chip's questions.

"Why, I suppose it's because I enjoy what I'm doing," he finally replied, stroking the fine wood he'd been shaping with a router.

"I wanted to take woodworking in school last year," Chip confided, "But the computer said the class was full and put me in metal shop instead."

"I could teach you woodworking right here," Harold offered. "I've got all the tools and plenty of wood—and there's no computer to tell us what to do," he added with a grin.

"Would you, really?" asked Chip, his enthusiasm showing through his usual cool demeanor.

Within a few weeks, Chip was working happily with Harold on the house and was even planning to make Christmas presents for his friends and family. He had also started to go to school again regularly because Harold had flatly refused to work with him if he continued to cut his classes.

"It's good to know how to work with your hands," the old man told him, "but you still need school to sharpen up your mind."

Both Chip's parents were amazed at the difference in his attitude. Although he never became a top student, he did graduate from high school, and through Harold's contacts he got a job as a cabinet maker's apprentice. Today, Chip is on his way to becoming a master cabinet maker—and he whistles while he works.

Yours, Mine—and Ours

When a teenager gets a chance to interact with more people on a regular daily basis, home may cease to be such a drag, especially when there are younger children to take care of and relate to, other adults to talk to and to bounce ideas off, or a senior citizen who tells fascinating tales of days gone by. If you can raise a child from the beginning in an environment that includes a diversity of people, so much the better; but if you already have a teenager who's been raised in a nuclear family (especially a single-parent nuclear family) or who is an only child, and you see him or her drifting aimlessly, perhaps it's time to try group housekeeping.

It's true that most kids will probably feel overwhelmed and confused at first, and may be resentful of the apparent or real intrusion of others into their lives, but they usually adapt to the new situation with surprising rapidity and enthusiasm. Chances are that within a short time you will probably see some very positive changes in attitude, a spirit of cooperativeness, the willingness to spend time at home, and a growing sense of responsibility.

We are familiar with several very successful group households consisting of one parent with a teenage child or children and another parent with children that are between two and seven years old. In a way, these households have recreated situations similar to those halcyon days when the older children in large families were expected to look after the younger ones. In the process, those children gained a sense of responsibility and accomplishment that many of today's teenagers never experience.

Virginia Nelson, Dora Tranz, and their respective children have been sharing a group household in which this type of arrangement has worked well for a couple of years. When Virginia divorced her husband and took sole custody of their two children, who were then three and five years old, she began to share her house with Dora, who is almost ten years her senior. Dora's son Brent was then fifteen years old.

Dora had been divorced for six years but had just made a career change and needed to cut back on expenses and to somehow find the time to devote herself as completely as possible to her work. Her new job required her to travel a bit and Brent presented a problem. She knew that he was too old to accept a baby-sitter, but she felt that he was too young to stay by himself, although Brent protested, "I can stay alone, Mom! You think I'm just a kid. You don't give me enough credit!" Dora felt she also couldn't rely on Brent's ability or willingness to find friends to stay with every time she had to go out of town. She hoped that a group living situation would mean that her son would not have to be left alone or in the care of strangers while she was away.

Initially, both Virginia and Dora had serious concerns about whether or not their individual families could live together happily. They liked each other and felt that they could get along without major problems, but they weren't sure how the age difference between their children would work out. Brent, an only child, had never been around younger children, even as a baby-sitter. His mother felt that the experience might be good for him, but she wasn't sure if he would see it that way, and she herself had reservations about whether she could handle the continual pressure of little children in her nonworking hours. She liked kids, but it had been quite a while since she'd had to put up with the deafening patter of little feet.

After much internal debate and a drastic lack of success in finding other suitable housemates, both Virginia and Dora decided to give it a try. They agreed to split the cooking and household chores as evenly as possible and assumed that the extra mess Virginia's kids might make would be balanced out by the periods when Dora traveled and Virginia had to assume full responsibility for the house. Happily, additional help arrived from an unexpected quarter:

Since the family motto was: Whoever doesn't cook does the dishes, Brent soon offered to learn to prepare a meal or two so that he could avoid having to do most of the dishes while his mother was away on one of her first trips. Virginia was happy to oblige, and after a little coaching, Brent was turning out some lovely salads and pasta dishes. When his mother returned, he proudly displayed his new talents and was promptly hailed as "a great new culinary expert." Not only did he gain a valuable survival skill, but he also received the kind of recognition and validation that young people thrive on— he was performing a vital function in the household, and doing it well.

Some of Brent's other adjustments weren't quite so easy to accomplish. At first, he clearly resented the presence of Virginia's two little children in his life. He felt that they were allowed to be much too noisy and rambunctious and protested that he had been much better behaved when he was younger (although his mother had somewhat different memories of him).

When Brent came home each afternoon, he would grumpily get himself a snack and closet himself in his room with the same TV programs he'd been watching alone for years, while his mother was away at work. Otherwise, he did his homework and kept pretty much to himself. He jealously kept the younger children away from his belongings and locked the door to his room whenever he went out.

In spite of this, little Stephen and Mara practically worshiped the ground Brent walked on. They were thrilled and fascinated by the "real big boy" who had come to live in their house. They couldn't have been more pleased if Ronald MacDonald himself had moved in. When Brent rode his bike up the driveway after school, they ran to meet him, greeted him with shrills of excitement, gazed with awe and envy at his ten-speed, fought over the privilege of carrying his books, and practically clung to his legs all the way into the house. Now, hero worship is powerful stuff. It would have taken a completely callous soul to withstand the power of their unbounded admiration. Little by little, Brent began to warm up to the kids, although he still refused to play with them or to baby-sit for them. That, he felt, was beneath him.

The crucial blow to his tower of resistance came one evening after dinner. Little Stephen had been unusually quiet throughout the meal, glancing thoughtfully at Brent every once in a while. Obviously, something was on his mind. When Brent left the table and walked into the living room, Stephen followed him and finally gained Brent's attention by tugging on his shirt.

"What do you want?" Brent asked somewhat irritably.

There was a pause while Stephen figured out how to phrase his request. "Will you be my big brother?" he finally asked, eyes round with seriousness and intensity.

"Mine too!" chimed in Mara, who had pursued them into the living room. "Be my big brother, too!"

Brent looked at the two of them in utter disbelief. Then he started to smile. "OK . . . I guess so . . . Sure!" He was immediately overwhelmed with hugs and kisses, which he fought off quite halfheartedly.

In the months that followed, all three children thrived on their new relationship as adopted brothers and sister even more than their mothers had dreamed possible. Things didn't always go smoothly between them, but then, that doesn't happen with natural siblings either. The little kids quieted down a bit when they found that their older brother needed some peace and quiet so he could study, and Brent began to spend some time watching television with his two little pals cuddled on the bed with him.

One night, when Virginia mentioned that she was looking for a baby-sitter, Brent offered to do the job. Virginia was happy to accept, but only if Brent would agree to the same payment as her usual sitter. Virginia knew that it was very important for him to know that she valued his time and services as much as an adult's, and that the fact that he shared his home with her children did not mean that he was obligated to take care of them. This is a crucial point in any household that includes a teenager. It may not always be necessary to compensate them with money, but a fair trade of services is really important in order to motivate them to assume more responsibility.

The Deafening Patter of Little Feet . . .

As it turned out, Brent's mother, Dora, had more difficulty adjusting to Virginia's children than he did. She would come home exhausted, after a hard day's work, wanting nothing more than a chance to rest quietly until the tension of the day wore off. When she and Brent had lived alone, he usually respected this need and would simply greet her and then leave her alone for a bit of quiet time before dinner. Now when Dora entered the house each evening, longing for a chance to sit down, kick off her shoes, put her feet up, and read the paper, she often found herself in the midst of chaos. Stephen and Mara ran around, screaming and hollering, giggling and tussling, and generally creating such pandemonium that Dora began to wish she were back in her nice, quiet office. Sometimes, the racket continued right through dinner until bedtime. By then, Dora's nerves were completely frazzled. Finally, she talked the problem over with Virginia.

"I know the kids aren't doing it to drive me crazy," she assured their mother. "And they aren't unusually ill-behaved either. There are evenings when they are quiet and considerate, and I want you to know that, on the whole, I think they are well-mannered, friendly, responsive, intelligent children. It's just that I can't handle their energy level when I get home from work and they are tearing up the house."

Reassured by Dora's opinion that her kids were not simply unruly, spoiled brats, Virginia found herself quite willing and eager to do what she could to deal with the problem. She tried feeding the children early and having them in the tub by the time Dora came home, but although Mara soon dropped off to sleep quietly enough, Stephen remained as wild as ever. He had always been a high-energy, easily irritated child, and by late afternoon he was literally in such a tizzy that his momentum often carried his sister along with him into a frenzy of activity that often ended unhappily for one or both of them. Virginia had always considered him a handful, and had simply learned to cope, but now that Stephen's behavior was causing problems in an otherwise highly satisfying living arrangement, she felt determined to look into the problem more closely. Luckily, a friend of Dora's came to visit one evening and supplied the solution to the problem.

"He behaves just as my son used to," she said. "We really had a terrible time with him before we found out what was causing it."

Both Dora and Virginia were all attention. "What was it?" they asked, "and how did you settle him down?"

"My son was what is known as a hyperactive child. It has to do with the way he assimilates food. We found that some things pepped him up, and other things calmed him down. Once we got his diet straightened out, he became much easier to live with. Like Stephen, he was always a lovely, friendly kid, but he'd just get so hyped up he didn't know what to do with his energy."

She suggested that they read Ruben Feingold's book, *Why Your Child Is Hyperactive*, which Dora and Virginia eagerly perused together. After all, Stephen might be Virginia's son, but they both had a lot to lose if he continued to raise havoc every evening. They made a concerted effort to identify and eliminate the foods from Stephen's diet that seemed to be causing his hyperactivity, and within a few weeks, their evenings became much quieter and more pleasant. Not only that, his teacher soon reported that he was much more attentive and less easily distracted in school. So because of Dora's presence in the house, Virginia was given the opportunity to come in contact with someone who had the key to her son's problem, and was able to take the necessary steps to deal with it. And because Dora wanted very much to continue what was otherwise a very satisfactory living arrangement, she was motivated to provide the support and assistance that her housemate needed.

There were other rewards for Dora as well. She began to find herself gaining a satisfaction and sense of fulfillment that she hadn't felt in years. She found herself becoming more and more interested in listening to Virginia talk about her children, and when Virginia was tired or sick, she took pleasure in reading them a bedtime story and tucking them in. Although she was much more strict with them than their mother was, they seemed to accept the difference with equanimity. Gradually, Dora began to assume the role of "other parent" in the household, a role that is quite similar to that of many fathers. She went off to work each day and came back in the evening, while Virginia operated a small business out of the house. Dora and her son did most of the yard work and a lot of the repair and maintenance that is usually done by the man of the house, while Virginia preferred indoor cleanups and clearly was the best cook. Dora also happened to be older and more experienced, and she often handled the bill paying and was generally deferred to for business decisions that affected the household.

When Dora and the Virginia realized that their roles
were developing along the traditional lines for husbands
and wives, they were quite amused. But since things
were working out quite well, they decided to let things
be the way they were and see what happened. Evidently,
Stephen and Mara thought things were working out just
fine, too, because one evening, as Dora was tucking them
into bed, Mara looked up at her and said, "My brother
and I talked it over and we want to keep you as a spare
mother."

"She's Not My Sister, We Just Live Together"

This showstopper was uttered by a thirteen-year-old boy
to a little old lady who had commented on how nice he
and his fifteen-year-old "big sister" looked, all dressed
up and waiting with a group of adults to enter a nice
restaurant for a birthday dinner. The boy played innocent at first, but later confessed that he had made the
statement for its shock value (the old lady had been sat-
isfyingly flabbergasted), and also because he "kind of
resented" the fact that everyone assumed he was a "little
brother" just as he was becoming a man. Whenever you
put a group of people together—any group—there's
bound to be some problems. One of the best ways to
keep these things from reaching major proportions is to
anticipate them and prepare yourself to deal with them
before they occur. Consequently, the rest of this chapter
is a troubleshooting guide to identifying and dealing
with some of the difficulties that can arise when children
are involved in group living situations.

How to Listen to the Dragon without Getting Burned

When Resentment, Jealousy, Anger, and Frustration rear their ugly heads, they can turn a nice person (of any age) into a ugly dragon. As we've noted before, one way to avoid a lot of this negativity is to create a household without children who are too close to one another in age. However, if and when a dragon rears its ugly head anyway (and we don't know of any household that is totally free of them—or any office or social situation either, for that matter!), the best way we've found to deal with it is called "active listening." This P.E.T. (that's Parent Effectiveness Training) technique is a good tool for any human being to develop, and here's how it works:

When people are exploding with negative and potentially destructive emotions, the best way to defuse them is to listen to them carefully, with obvious and sincere interest, but without making any judgments or suggestions. People who are upset really need to be listened to, need to know that you know that they are hurting, frustrated, or angry. Usually, at that point, they are not of a mind to listen to your opinions anyway, so just saying, "I really hear you. You must be feeling very angry right now. That really was frustrating, no wonder you're upset," can be much more useful in getting people to a place where they've experienced and expressed their emotions and are now ready to deal with their problems effectively. This technique is especially effective with children. They must be allowed to express their emotions and have those emotions validated or they will tend to repress them or get out of touch with themselves. As long as they receive affection, understanding, and support—rather than criticism and judgment—they will usually be willing to adjust to a new situation with grace

161

and charm you never dreamed they possessed, once the
initial agony is over. Remember, your children have
managed to adjust to an enormous variety of new experiences ever since they were born. In fact, they may
be our best indication of the almost infinite capacity for
adjustment that has allowed us puny, hairless, clawless,
blunt-toothed creatures to survive on this planet when
a lot of the big guys became extinct. So, chances are, if
you can manage to listen patiently and attentively to
their troubles, your children will eventually see for
themselves that they are gaining more than they are losing in their new living situation and life will settle down
to a day-to-day existence that may be more rewarding
than any they've experienced previously.

"Fine," you say, "but how many saints can sit and listen 'patiently and attentively' while their kids are
screaming with anger and blaming them for thrusting
them into this new and frustrating situation?" The key
here is not to get hooked into feeling guilty because your
child is feeling resentment toward you for creating the
situation. You are doing the best you can to create a living
arrangement that provides the things both you and your
child need to live a happy life. You are doing it out of
love and necessity. There is nothing to feel guilty about.
If you find that you do anyway, then talk it out with
someone. Don't let it fester and control the way you deal
with your children—nothing could be more destructive.
If you know you've done what you think and feel is the
best possible thing, then rely on that knowledge to keep
you in a place where you can hear their complaints without feeling attacked or guilty. It is important for children
to be able to express their feelings, and often they may
have some surprising insights to share that may help you
to arrange things even more satisfactorily in the long run.
The key is communication. By all concerned. And true

communication is a two-way thing—you have to listen to each other if what you say is to have any impact at all.

OK, now that you've got the "all-purpose, handy-dandy dragon-slaying technique" down, let's talk about some of the major and minor situations that awaken those dragons within us.

Manipulation: "Jimmy's Daddy Lets Me Do It, So Why Don't You?"

When children begin to play off one adult in a household against another, it can lead to bad feelings all around unless the channels of communication between the adults are flowing freely and they agree to make a joint effort to discover why the child feels the need to engage in such behavior. It is really important that every adult in the household be able to maintain his or her own integrity in deciding what kind of behavior will and will not be tolerated from the kids (with the child's parents being the final arbiters, of course). Children learn quite quickly just what different adults expect of them and how much they will tolerate from them, and this kind of sensitivity will prove to be more and more useful in the future. If they find that Uncle Frank is a much softer touch when it comes to ice cream sundaes than Mommy is, fine—everyone deserves a clandestine treat now and then. But they will also learn that Uncle Frank is very strict about food-throwing at the table, whereas Ginny sometimes joins in the fun, when the other grown-ups aren't around. The idea here is for the adults to be open with each other about what they will and will not tolerate, and to acknowledge that, in the long run, the parents of each child have the final say. Then the answer can simply be, "Jimmy's daddy makes his decisions and

163

I make mine. If you want to do it, do it when Jimmy's daddy can clean up the mess!"

Rebellion: "You're Not My Mommy! I Don't Have to Do What You Say!"

Sometimes a child will flatly refuse a request made by a housemate and will belligerently assert that the housemate has absolutely no right to make any requests at all. Here again, a solution will only emerge if the housemate and the child's parent take the opportunity to communicate with the child on the issue. After all, it's not fun to go from living with only one or two parents to a situation where you've suddenly got even more grown-ups giving the orders. So it's important to find out whether the child felt that the request was unfair and was looking for a plausible reason for refusing, if the child has found the housemate's behavior to be irritating or annoying for some reason and is not motivated to respond to any request at all, or if the child simply resents the housemate on general principles and needs to be reconciled to the fact that the housemate exists. Whatever the case, the idea is for the housemate to discuss the problem with the parent, for the parent to discuss it with the child, and then for all concerned to get together to work out something tha makes everyone feel better. As the child begins to feel understood and valued, rather than put down or ordered about, the rebellious behavior should begin to disappear.

Crushes: "Will You Marry Me When I Grow Up?"

Sometimes a young child will develop a crush on an older one, much to the embarrassment or annoyance of the beloved. If the older child can be helped to understand that the crush is really a compliment, and that he or she is under no obligation to return the affection at the same intensity, the potential problems in the situation will usually fade away as the younger child grows up and the status of the older child changes from being a new and exotic figure in the house to someone who is part of the family.

Having a teenager smitten with a crush on an older housemate can be a more serious problem, especially if the young girl or boy makes attempts at seduction. In these cases, the adult needs to be prepared to deal with the situation with tact and kindness, but *without* responding sexually.

Recently, our friend Jim began to wake up at night to find Kerry, the prematurely pubescent eleven-year-old daughter of his housemate, cuddled up naked in his bed. He was fully aware of the potentially compromising and downright illegal situation he was being placed in and was also worried about damaging the girl's self-confidence at such an important time in her life. How could he make it plain that there could be nothing physical between them without rejecting her as a female? There was no possibility of ignoring the situation, even if he took to locking his bedroom door, and he knew it was important that she get over her crush on him before it had an effect on her social life in the future.

Finally, he got up the nerve to consult the girl's mother about the situation, hoping that she would not be "freaked out" by her daughter's precocious behavior. To his surprise, the mother was very understanding.

"She's always been a hot little number," she said sympathetically. "I guess it's because she is maturing physically much earlier than girls usually do. But then, she has always been a snuggle-bug, who seemed to need a lot of kisses and hugs from everyone and was very free about giving them out. Please don't take it personally, I know that you've done nothing to encourage her."

Jim was relieved to find that he was not going to be hauled off as a child molester, and he and Kerry's mother discussed the best way to handle the situation. They both felt that it would probably be easiest on Kerry's ego if Jim talked the matter over with her in private, and her mother agreed to "discover the situation" and back him up if the initial talks failed to change Kerry's nocturnal behavior.

The next day, he asked Kerry to take a walk with him so they could talk in private. Then he told her that he liked her very much, as a person, and really enjoyed living in the same house as she did, but that the visits to his bed would have to stop. He talked to her seriously, as one adult to another, with friendly affection that gave her full credit for being old enough to understand what he was saying.

"It's not that I don't like having you near me. Everyone likes to cuddle up with someone; it feels good. But I am twenty-nine and you are eleven, and any kind of physical stuff between us is just out of the question."

"Why?" she asked with seductive innocence. "Because you think I'm just a baby?"

"Not at all," he replied. "I think you are a very attractive young lady, and I know that, as time goes on, you will become even more beautiful. I also know that you are not feeling like a baby, but very much like a woman. But, no matter what you think, you are just not emotionally ready for sex yet, and I am not emotionally prepared to have a love affair with someone your age."

"How do you know if you don't try it?" she asked.

"Well, for one thing, it's illegal. I could be sent to jail and branded as a pervert for sleeping with you. It would ruin my life and your reputation and would cause a lot of grief for your family, too. I really like living in your house. It has been a very happy home for me, and I don't want to jeopardize that in any way. I want to be able to go on living there, to be friends with you and with your folks, and to enjoy my life. Isn't that what you really want, too?"

Kerry thought it over. "I didn't know it was illegal," she said. Then an idea dawned. "Will you marry me when I grow up?" she asked.

"That's a long time from now," Jim replied kindly. "I have no idea what will happen to either of us in the future. We will both meet a lot of people and we may not even know each other by then. Besides, when you grow up, you will be a different person—and you may not even like me. Or, I may be married to someone else. No, I don't think I can promise to marry you in the future. But I am willing to be friends with you right now. No love stuff, just people together. What do you say?"

"You really want to be my friend? You're not just saying that to make me feel good?" Kerry asked, eyeing him suspiciously.

"I am already your friend," Jim said, "I always have been. Just because being lovers is out of the question has nothing to do with friendship. I think you're a really neat person, Kerry, and I'd enjoy taking a walk with you now and then, or catching a movie once in a while, as long as you understand where I'm coming from and get off the sex stuff."

"Well, all right," she agreed slowly. Then her eyes brightened. "There's a new boy in my school—a senior!

And I think he likes me! Do you know what he said to me the other day. . . ?"

As she chattered on, Jim heaved a sigh of relief knowing that, for the present anyway, the assault was over.

Jim handled the situation well by dealing with Kerry as a grown-up and not putting her down as a little girl. He managed to make it clear that he liked her a lot and found her to be an attractive person, while making it quite definite that his interest in her was not sexual, for some very *practical* reasons. He did not lead her on with vague hopes about the future, but he did offer a present relationship that they both could deal with and enjoy. Thus, he validated her as an individual, which did a great deal to soften whatever rejection was involved. In the ensuing months he was careful to maintain the boundaries of the friendship that he had offered. Every once in a while, Jim spent some time with Kerry, but he saw to it that those occurrences did not take place too often. He knew that a teenager who spends a great deal of really satisfying time with an older man or woman may find girls and boys of his or her own age less interesting than they would normally be. Jim encouraged Kerry to focus on her peer group for fun, and inquired about her latest school crushes with interest. In this way he made her feel good about herself and gave her the acceptance and affection she needed without taking her focus away from her own age group.

It helped a great deal for Jim to be able to talk it out with Kerry's mother first, since that removed the risk of being compromised. However, if he had felt that she was unable to accept what was going on, he probably would have simply dealt with Kerry directly and perhaps threatened to talk to her mother as a last resort if she kept climbing into his bed. Too often parents can become hysterical, accusing the hapless object of their child's affections as being in some way responsible. Or they can tease the child, who will then feel humiliated and betrayed. So it is important to weigh the natures of the individuals involved before tackling such a situation.

Sexual Experimentation Among Housemate Children: "If You'll Show Me Yours, I'll Show You Mine!"

All children engage in sexual experimentation at one time or another, with their own siblings, friends, or schoolmates. Fortunately, most of today's parents are not as uptight about this as parents were years ago. This kind of curiosity is now known to be a normal part of child development. But when two families are living together, and some children are much older than others, it sometimes happens that an older child who has never had the opportunity to examine a member of the opposite sex will develop an acute case of the "Peeping Toms" or will be caught taking a little child's panties down. Usually, this is not something to make a big fuss about, but it is important that it be dealt with properly. The older child's parent should take him or her aside and discuss the matter quietly and sympathetically. The child will need to be assured that there is nothing "sick" about his or her curiosity, but that the manner in which it is being expressed is not satisfactory. The issue should be discussed in terms of personal rights. Everyone has the right to exist without being used as instructional materials by someone else. "You wouldn't have liked it if an older kid did that to you, would you?" The child may respond gratefully to one of the books that are available that discuss sex and contain pictures of the way people of both sexes are built, and the parent should be willing to answer any questions that may arise. You can also share the fact that you used to be curious, too, and may have done the same thing when you were younger, and that you learned your lesson the hard way, too. In that way, everyone will come out of the situation with ego intact.

ADULTS MOLESTING CHILDREN: A MUCH MORE SERIOUS SITUATION

This is quite a different matter from children engaged in playing doctor. It is serious and should be treated as such. The best way to deal with it, of course, is to avoid it in the first place by carefully screening prospective housemates and by *never* repressing any suspicious feeling that *this* is a person who is not to be trusted alone with your child. You need not say anything, of course, but just pass that person over in your search for a housemate. There are plenty of normal, psychologically healthy adults in this world. You do not ever have to subject yourself or your children to living with one who isn't. If you miss, however, and you begin to suspect an existing roommate, your best protection is to have developed good communications with your child to begin with.

If a child is asked the right questions, in a non-panicky way, he or she will usually tell you exactly what's been going on and will be open to counseling and a warning not to submit to adult molestation. In this way, without compromising the person you suspect (because you may be wrong), the child will be able to avoid being exploited if such a situation should arise. The idea is to ask if anyone has made advances or tried to touch the child sexually, rather than to ask if a specific person has been guilty of such behavior. Another way to go about it is to ask what the child would do if someone were to behave in this manner and suggest that the proper response is to refuse to comply and to come to you immediately so that you can handle things. He or she should be informed that there are people in the world who are attracted to children, that such people are usually not evil but that to agree to such proposals is out of the question. In that way, the child can be spared the fright or guilt that such an encounter can bring, and will be reassured that you are there to prevent any further occurrences.

If such a thing does happen to your child, the offending adult should be quickly and quietly turned over to the authorities, and no guilt trips should be laid on the child. There is nothing to be gained from trying to deal with the person yourself; such problems can only be dealt with by professionals. Simply asking the person to leave will only set him or her free to make attempts on someone else's kids.

CHILD ABUSE: A MATTER THAT IS EVERYBODY'S BUSINESS

Although parents should usually be free to discipline their children as they see fit, child abuse is quite another matter. If it occurs in any living situation, get in touch with the authorities *immediately*. They will usually arrange to keep the offending person away from the child or children until proper steps can be taken to deal with this type of illness and its effects. *Never ignore such actions.* By ignoring or excusing a parent or other adult who beats, burns, or otherwise mistreats a child, you are contributing to that child's psychological and physical abuse. You are adding to that child's sense of helplessness, the sense that he or she is trapped in an impossible situation, and that no one can help. There is a great deal of enlightened counseling available for child abusers, but most of them are not willing to admit that they need help. The tendency is to justify the abuse or to reassure oneself that it will never happen again. If you aren't sure what to do about the situation, get in touch with a local family counseling center or a professional psychologist and follow their instructions to the letter. There are also "hotlines" and "crisis centers" in many communities to handle such emergencies.

"I Can't Handle This Now, Let's Discuss It on Thursday"

As you can see from the topics covered in this chapter, most of the problems involved in group living situations with children closely parallel the problems that can arise in any family. And in any family, success in dealing with such issues depends on a policy of open communication among everyone involved. That is why we urge you to hold a family meeting on a weekly basis at which all housemembers, young or old, can have the opportunity to air their grievances, ask their questions, state their needs, and make their requests in a safe, friendly setting. By getting together regularly, you can really turn a house into a home and develop the sensitivity to one another that can make group housekeeping a wonderful experience.

CHAPTER VIII

A Family of Friends

As we have said many times throughout this book, the way to avoid problems and misunderstandings with the other members of your household (and with any other people, for that matter) is to be very clear about your agreements with them and open about your feelings when disagreements occur. We've worked out a sample Household Agreement that covers what we think are the vital points and we offer it to you at the end of this chapter for use in creating a written agreement for your particular situation and housemates. Ideally, these agreements should be worked out by all the people in a household before they begin to live together. Of course if your home is running successfully on a previously written agreement you may simply want to ask each new housemate to sign and conform to the agreement as a condition of moving into the house. However, nothing is written in stone, and even a basic Household Agreement can and should be changed as circumstances change in the household. To do this, and to settle any other dispute as well, a family meeting is a necessity.

GETTING TO KNOW YOU

As you have probably gathered from much of the fore-going, we feel that regular household meetings are the key to turning a house into a home and for transforming a group of strangers into a family of friends. Not only are these sessions vital for preventing and solving most of the problems and issues that arise in any group household by providing a forum for a fair hearing and a democratic decision, but they also bring the members of your extended family closer to one another by providing the opportunity for communication and understanding in a relatively free, nonjudgmental atmosphere. We learned the practice from family counselors, and although our marriages ended, the family conferences remained as an important part of our relationships with our children and eventually with our housemates.

To work most efficiently, these household get-togeth-ers should occur at least once a week and should be structured into the household routine as a regularly scheduled feature. Attendance should be mandatory. The secret to success where these meetings are concerned is one of *attitude*. They should not be seen as gripe sessions or as political arenas in which to take sides on household issues, but rather as a chance to spend some time as a family unit and find ways to make life more pleasant for everyone in the house.

Aside from financial considerations, most people who join group households are looking for companionship, but since most of us live on different and busy schedules, we often find ourselves merely coexisting, meeting as briefly in the hall and in the dining room as strangers on a train. This is ample reason for everyone in the house to look forward to a quiet weekly get-together and a chance to talk things over, bring each other up to date on current triumphs and tragedies, and voice and solve any problems that may have come up.

These meetings should take place at a preselected, mutually convenient time. Although you can linger for hours if you like, the "business" portion of the meeting should be planned for no less than half an hour and no more than two hours to provide ample time to give each issue the attention it deserves and to prevent filibustering. We repeat: Attendance should be mandatory, and this should be part of any agreement between a prospective roommate and the other members of the household.

There will be occasions, of course, when a household member cannot make a meeting—but this should not be allowed to become a habit. In our experience, a person who chronically misses meetings is either trying to avoid being taken to task for transgressions or is simply unable to confront other people directly. Such people are generally difficult to live with anyway. To make it much harder for anyone to get away with "Oh, I forgot," we suggest that you make every effort to schedule your meetings on the same day of each week, at a time convenient to everyone in the house, and be willing to change the meeting to accommodate changes in individual schedules owing to work and classes. Then make an agreement that missing three meetings in a row constitutes giving notice of departure from the household (unless someone is out of town for an extended stay).

Every type of conference needs some kind of leadership and mediation, and you can either rotate as chairpeople or choose one person who does it really well and let that person run the meeting each week, unless someone else requests the honor. If there is no major household crisis taking place, many extended families allow each of the school-age children in the household to have a turn as leader along with the adults. Not only is this excellent experience for the kids, but it is often educational for the grown-ups as well, since children are often able to come directly (and often disconcertingly) to the heart of a matter without pussyfooting around.

The meeting should be structured but informal. There is no need to employ *Roberts' Rules of Order*, but old business should be finished before new business is started, and each member of the household should be given a chance to introduce issues and to speak his or her mind on the matters at hand. Decisions should be made democratically once the options have been evaluated, either by open or closed vote depending on the sensitivity of the issue.

How to Disagree Agreeably

Every member of the household should agree to take the attitude that you have come together to solve problems rather than to make complaints, demand restitutions, and exact punishments. Since nobody wants to be the house leper, it is pretty certain that most people will do what they can to remedy inadvertent (let's give them the benefit of the doubt) blunders. So, be diplomatic. As many people have learned in human potential training, it is far better to say, "I feel very upset when you leave your dirty dishes in the sink until they grow mold," than to point a trembling finger and shout, "You're a slob!" The first method opens the way for the miscreant to do something to help you (like cleaning up immediately), while the second puts the culprit on the defensive, which leads to anger, which leads to more dirty dishes.

The key is to listen to one another, no matter how high emotions may be running. Even though you don't agree, you may be able to get in touch with your opponent's reality and find a creative way to give both of you what you need, or at least to compromise. Try to resolve most issues at the meeting unless everyone feels that time may do more to heal things than a swift decision. If this is the case, check on how things have turned out during the old-business segment of the next meeting.

In most instances, being the focus of a complaint from one or all of the members of the household should be enough to cause the miscreant to mend his or her ways. But, if a housemate fails to correct the situation, the next time it comes up there should be some sanctions reached by democratic vote. This can be extra work for the house goldbrick (such as weeding the lawn or cleaning the oven), the absorption of late-payment charges by the late payer who held the bill up past its due date, or downright eviction for a habitual slipper-and-slider.

Although the most successful households are often the least rigid, there is one issue, however, where there can be absolutely no Mickey Mousing around: the rent! Paying the rent in full and paying it on time should not be a negotiable matter, regardless of the circumstances. After all, the primary reason most of you are living to-gether is to share the cost of putting the roof over your heads and that must be viewed as the prime responsi-bility and priority by all concerned. It is unthinkable to place your housemates in a position where they can be evicted from their home if they don't cough up your share of the rent on time. Therefore, it should be under-stood by all concerned before they move into the house that roommates who are delinquent more frequently than once in six months will be asked to leave the house.

If you hit a period of bad luck, it would be better to stash the rent money for the next month or two in a safe place and beg or borrow food and carfare than to be delinquent on the rent. It is one thing to carry someone's share of the food until his or her fortunes improve, it is quite another to pay more than one's share of the monthly rental. This may seem unduly harsh, but it is vitally necessary. It is difficult to oust a roommate who is out of work and having trouble finding employment. But if the other roommates shoulder the rent burden, they may cut the delinquent's motivation to find a new job—any new job—in order to survive. And, if there isn't enough money to keep everyone afloat, everyone in the house will end up going down with the ship together.

The Pros and Cons of Using a Suggestion Box

Households that include individuals who feel that they cannot confront one another directly on certain issues sometimes deposit their gripes or requests in a suggestion box, which is then opened at the family meeting. Because some of the suggestions are anonymous, it takes a vote by everyone to act on them. The positive side of such a method is that it gives the shy members of the household a chance to air views they fear may be unpopular. The negative side of it is that it prevents the members of the household from learning to confront each other honestly, and it can be used spitefully for poison pen notes. If you do use such a box, we suggest you keep it locked to prevent people from removing notes they put in during the heat of the moment and have second thoughts about later. By thus ensuring spontaneity, you get the benefits of expressing your anger when it is fresh—and you can always say, "I was really upset when I wrote that, but I am no longer angry with you now," and give your housemates a valuable clue to what bugs you and to the fact that you are willing to forgive and forget.

GETTING IT ALL DOWN ON PAPER

The leitmotif that runs throughout all of the foregoing is *agreement*. You have probably noticed that time and again we have urged you to get things settled before problems start, to present issues and gain approval before a roommate moves in. To do this, it is vitally necessary that you come up with a written Household Agreement that every prospective roommate must sign before moving in. The benefits of such a procedure are numerous: A written agreement provides prospective housemates with a clear and accurate picture of the requirements of being part of the household. Nobody can say, "You didn't tell me I couldn't bring my ocelot." It also assures each member of the household a fair and equitable share of the space, expenses, and work. It lays down the rules of conduct in a reasonable manner, so that infringements can be discussed rationally, without anyone's saying, "I didn't know I couldn't play my stereo after 10 P.M., and I can't study without it." (The answer to that one, by the way, is headphones.)

What should your Household Agreement contain? The best way to show you is by example, so here's a sample agreement that you can modify to suit the needs and circumstances of your particular situation:

HOUSEHOLD AGREEMENT

We, the members of the household residing at 12 Mockingbird Lane, Saratoga, California, do hereby agree to abide by the

179

following for as long as we each shall continue to be a member of the household:

I. Rent:
   A. The rent for each month shall be divided as follows:
      1. $400 for the master bedroom and private bathroom
      2. $300 for each of the other bedrooms and shared baths
   B. Each household member will pay his or her last month's rent in advance, as well as a $100 cleaning and security deposit. This deposit will be returned if the individual leaves the premises in good condition. The last month's rent will be forfeited if the person fails to give thirty days' notice. (Any housemate who is asked to leave will be given thirty days' notice.)
   C. If any household member leaves or is asked to leave and a new housemate is not found within thirty days, the other members will divide that portion of the rent among them until a new housemate is found. [NOTE: In a case where one person owns the house and simply rents out rooms, that person would usually absorb the deficit until a new renter was found.]
   D. There is a $50 per month reduction in rent for mowing, watering, and weeding the lawn and gardens. Gloria has agreed to take on this responsibility.

II. Utilities:
   A. The gas, electricity, water and sewage, refuse collection, and cable TV bills will be divided equally among the household members.
   B. Joe will serve as Keeper of the Bible, post monthly work schedules, collect rent and utilities payments, pay the bills and do other household accounting work, in return for which he will be excused from other monthly duties.

C. Any household member who is late in paying utilities will be required to pay the late-payment charges for the bills in question.

III. Telephone:

Each member of the household shall provide his or her own telephone service using the existing jacks and instruments if available, or providing and installing them at his or her own cost.

[or]

The basic telephone charges will be divided equally between the members of the household, who will furnish their own instruments and jacks if necessary. A telephone log will be kept next to the hall phone and all long-distance calls will be logged into it, immediately after each call has been completed, including the area code and number dialed, the date, and the time the call was initiated.

IV. Parking:

The two garage spaces will be rotated on a monthly basis among household members in alphabetical order by last name, with all other vehicles to be parked on the street. A garage parking schedule will appear in the "Bible." Any housemate who blocks entry or exit to the garage will be fined $5.

V. Sharing Chores:

Each household member agrees to do a fair share of the daily, weekly, and monthly upkeep of the premises. Joe will post a schedule of such chores in the "Bible" and on the kitchen bulletin board.

VI. Distribution of Space:

Each household member is entitled to equal storage space; adequate access to the bathroom, kitchen, and common areas; and to the privacy of his or her own bedroom. Complaints and adjustments can be dealt with at family meetings.

VII. Guests:

    A. Overnight guests are permitted to share a household member's bedroom on a short-term basis only. All members of the household must agree before a guest is allowed to stay for more than three nights, or on the living room sofa.

    B. It is the responsibility of the host or hostess to inform guests of household rules and to feed and clean up after them.

    C. Guests who make themselves objectionable to other household members may be asked not to return.

VIII. Family Meetings:

    A. All members of the household agree to get together on Mondays at 6 P.M. for a minimum of forty-five minutes to discuss the happenings of the week, make announcements, air complaints, and settle disputes.

    B. A locked complaint box will be kept under the kitchen bulletin board so that problems can be noted as they come up. This box will be opened each week at the family meeting.

    C. The essence of a happy house is communication, and the object of each family meeting will be to keep the wheels of communication well-greased and in good repair. Therefore, all housemates who cannot attend a meeting must inform the others of that in advance. Any housemate who misses two meetings in a row will be fined $20, three consecutive absences will result in probation as a household member, and four will result in automatic notice of eviction (unless mitigating circumstances exist).

IX. Noise:

    A. Because of thin walls and varying schedules, all house members agree to be considerate of their housemates when playing televisions, stereos, musical instruments, and in keeping the noise level down, in general.

B. Quiet time begins after 10 P.M., but can be requested at other times by housemates for personal reasons.

C. Constant noise offenders will be fined an amount to be decided upon at a family meeting.

X. "Fine Times" Box:

All fines will be placed in a "Fine Times" box, to be kept by the Keeper of the Bible, and all monies therein will be used for household parties or to buy things for the common use of household members.

XI. Members of the Household:

A. All existing household members must agree unanimously on the acquisition of any new pet or the admission of a new housemate.

B. All problems involving existing pets or housemates should be aired at the family meeting.

C. If four or five housemates agree that a pet or person is no longer compatible with the group, that pet or person may be asked to leave on thirty days notice. [NOTE: This clause of the agreement would be different if one person owns the house and rents the rooms to the others. In this case, the owner should have the final say on all pets and housemates. However, for the sake of peace and harmony it would be wise for the owner to try for general agreement on additions to and subtractions from the household.]

XII. Leaving the Household:

A. All members of this household promise to provide a forwarding address when they move.

B. The outgoing members' share of the bills and charges incurred during their final month in residence will be deducted from their cleaning and security deposit.

C. All members of this household promise to leave the premises clean and in good repair. If they fail to do so, the cost of repairing any damage they may have caused and the cost of employing professional help to clean and restore their room will be deducted from the cleaning and security deposit, and if more funds are required they will be responsible for providing them.

D. The balance of the cleaning and security deposit will be returned to the departing member of the household when all of the above conditions have been satisfied and no later than thirty days after their last day in residence.

XIII. Extended Family Commitment:

All members of this household are committed to doing everything in their power to make this house a happy, supportive, and attractive place to live. To this end, we will respect one another, treat one another with generosity and consideration, communicate freely and sympathetically, and do our best to create a family environment for all concerned.

Signed: Date:

Remember that this *sample* agreement should be altered to suit the circumstances in your household. Many group households run quite well on simple and informal arrangements—especially when just two people are living together. However, even if you feel that you don't need as elaborate an agreement as we've provided, we urge you to at least have your prospective housemate read this one and point out any concepts that would be unacceptable. This is a good quick way to check compatibility and similarity of life-styles and attitudes toward responsibility. And even if you feel that you will be able to live quite happily without any but the most informal arrangements, be sure to write those down and have everyone sign them. If you are turned off by the need for such formalities, then turn it into a pleasant ritual—with candlelight and a little dinner—before the new person moves in. There is nothing wrong with having a ceremony to honor a commitment to live together in peace and harmony—after all, people have been holding weddings for years!

Now that you know how to keep things harmonious at home, it is time to talk about those aspects of group living that come under legal rules and regulations. In the next chapter, we explore what happens when the members of an existing or planned group household encounter "the powers that be."

CHAPTER IX

Staying on the Right Side
of the Law

We hope that by now you're feeling really enthusiastic at the prospect of sharing your living space with other people. There are so many positive aspects to group living: saving money, sharing the workload, and improving your social life, to name a few. We're repeating this "commercial" because it is time for us to discuss a couple of negative issues that may crop up when you set up a group household, and we don't want you to change your mind because of them. After all, there are positive and negative sides to everything in this world, and the best way to handle a hassle is to anticipate it and avoid it if you can. And if you can't, it sure helps to know what to expect. With this in mind, let's get down to some of the ways that your friendly local and state government can make things difficult for a group household.

Bureaucratic creativity being what it is, the rules, restrictions, and regulations covering zoning, building codes, and unrelated people living together vary widely from town to town, county to county, and state to state. Therefore, although we will do our best to give you an idea of what legal mumbo jumbo you might run up

against, you will have to do the legwork in your area to
see whether any laws or codes apply to your situation.
Please remember that these are only possibilities and
that none of them may give you any trouble at all. In
most cases, the fact that a few people have decided to
live quietly together in a house or an apartment creates
no problems for anyone concerned. It is only when a
large number of people want to share a single-family
residence (more than five, for instance) or when two or
more people decide to build or buy a house together,
that the long arm of the law reaches into their lives.

A Boarding House Is Not a Home!

If you own a house and want to rent rooms to a couple
of people, you probably can go ahead and do just that
without running afoul of the law. Most zoning restrictions that apply are designed to prevent people from setting up boarding houses in residential neighborhoods
and to prevent others from dividing up larger homes into
several apartments, thereby "commercializing" the
neighborhood. As long as you don't do any major alterations to the house and don't rent rooms to an entire band
of gypsies (although that might be fun!), you can probably take people into your home without any legal problems at all. A group household is neither a boarding
house nor a hotel nor an apartment buiding. Just a few
individuals who don't happen to be blood relations sharing living space.

To be on the safe side, try calling your local Zoning
Department. You can find it in the "Government" section of your phonebook. Without giving them your name,
tell them that you are planning to share your house with
other people and ask if any restrictions apply. Tell them

how many people you'd like to add to your household, and make it very clear that it would not be a commercial operation, just sharing extra space with some roommates. Since the difference between a commercial boarding house and a group household is that the former is a money-*making* operation and the latter is a money-*saving* operation, be sure that they understand that you are not making a profit on the deal—just splitting up the cost of living among several people. (If it turns out that you do come out ahead financially by renting these rooms, do not spread this joyous news to the Zoning Department!) Should you find yourself being drawn into the bureaucratic maze, just keep stressing that the people you intend to take into your home will not be tenants, they will be housemates. Listen to whatever information the department has to offer, and if it seems complicated, drop in and pick up printed copies of the data. They might mail the information to you if you are willing to give them your name and address.

RENTING SOMEONE ELSE'S SPACE

It is somewhat easier to share rented space with other people. In most areas, unless you are contemplating living with five or more people, no zoning restrictions should apply. However, you do have one important factor to consider, and that is the landlord. Check your lease carefully to ascertain that you are allowed to sublet space in your apartment and that there are no restrictions on the number of people who can live there. Note that sublet clauses generally refer to cases where you move out of the apartment and rent it to someone else instead of turning it back to the landlord. Since many landlords like to raise the rent when new tenants arrive, and also like to have a say in who will be renting their real estate, they can be understandably thorny on this issue. However, because you intend to go on living in the apartment or house, this kind of sublet clause is not applicable. So when you look at your lease, look for restrictions on subletting to additional people rather than those that deal with subletting in your absence.

If your lease has no such restrictions and you intend to take in some housemates, you will have to decide whether or not to let your landlord know what you are doing. This is where most people split into two factions: Those whose motto is "Honesty is the best policy," and those who firmly believe in "Don't make waves!" If your relationship with your landlord is friendly, we urge you to take him or her into your confidence. If you rent from a large corporation, or if your landlord resides in China and has not set foot on the property in many years, you might want to let well enough alone and keep mum. Only you can make this decision. While you're making it, be sure to consider your neighbors, too. If the neighborhood tattletale tells on you, you're not going to look too good when the landlord comes around to investigate rumors of strangers living communally at your house.

Your Home Is Your Castle—Unless You Want to Remodel It . . .

If you are planning to alter your house in order to rent out a couple of rooms, be aware that you will have to budget in additional time, money, and aggravation in order to thread your way through the local building codes. The nature and extent of this procedure varies greatly with the locality. When Deanna wanted to build a tiny carport, she ended up having to go through the

City Planning Commission, the Architectural Review
Board, and the Building and Zoning Departments in
order to get permission to do so. It took three days to
build the carport—and a year to get through the legal
tangle! When it was over, she'd spent $850 on materials
and labor—and $350 in fees, photos, and blueprints, not
to mention days of work lost in order to sit through hearings. Not only were there restrictions on where she could
build, but also on the architectural style, building materials, even the color paint she could use and the kind
of landscaping involved. To add a bit of salt to her
wounds, she found out that if she had bought a house
two blocks away, outside the city limits, none of these
restrictions would have applied. Under county jurisdic-
tion in her area, you can do pretty much anything you
please, as long as it doesn't fall down when someone's
looking.

So before you rush headlong to the do-it-yourself center because you intend to turn that extra closet into a
bathroom, or the garage into extra living space, weigh
the project carefully to be sure it will be worth the effort.
And before you buy so much as a nail, make sure you
know every step that will have to be taken to keep the
government out of your hair. Which brings us to a helpful
section on—

How to Make Friends with the Administrative Mind

The easiest way to deal with the local building bureau-
cracy is to let someone else do your dealing for you. Although it is tempting to undertake renovations yourself,
or to hire a cut-rate carpenter who will do the job for
peanuts, there is much to be said for placing the job in

the hands of a licensed contractor, and even for calling in an architect, if extensive alterations are involved or if you live in an especially restrictive area.

Contractors generally are more expensive than independent workers, but they will undertake all the paperwork for you and will be responsible for getting the job done in a way that will satisfy all the local ordinances and building codes. Because they spend a great deal of their time dealing with the administrators involved, they generally are much more successful at cutting through the red tape.

Architects, too, can save you money by designing structures that make economic use of space and building materials, and that are safe, legal, and attractive, as well. Whether you decide to use professional help or to do the whole thing yourself, be sure that whatever you do conforms to the building codes and is done with the proper permits. Even if your project "meets code," if you complete it without a building permit, you may find yourself in very hot water at a later date. Many people who try to sell houses find themselves forced to tear down or redo areas that were built illegally before they can get proper financing and clear escrow.

If you decide to do the job without a contractor, you will have to deal with the people in the various departments who control the paperwork you need. Although much has been said about the administrative mind and petty bureaucrats, we've found that many people in such positions are really quite human—if you approach them in the proper way. Because their jobs consist of getting in the way of other people's business, they are used to being viewed negatively. Therefore, the most disarming thing you can do is to come in with a positive attitude. You can always be paranoid later, if things get rough!

Here are some tried and true suggestions for dealing with the people behind the desks:

1. *Be friendly, cheerful, and pleasant.* Behave as though you expect them to do everything they can to be helpful.

2. *Be coherent.* Come prepared to explain what it is you want to do. If you can, bring sketches and samples of the materials you want to use. You don't need elaborate blueprints for simple jobs, often a clear sketch will fill the bill nicely. On this first visit they will tell you whether they need more formal documentation, and what the rules of the game are.

3. *Be respectful.* These people deal with building projects every day. They know a great deal. They are tired of being treated like robots and prefer to be treated like experts. So ask their advice and listen to what they have to say. If you can get someone in the Building Department interested in the creative beginnings of your project, you may have a valuable friend when it comes time to get final approval at the end of it.

4. *Be careful not to say too much.* Ninety percent of the trouble people get into with civil servants usually comes as a result of running off at the mouth. As Jack Webb used to say, "Just give the facts. Nothing but the facts." With this is mind, if you are planning an alteration in order to establish a group household, keep that to yourself. All the Building Department needs to know is that you want some extra space. And don't chat about the other projects you've done around the house, unless they were covered by building permits.

5. *Be practical rather than emotional.* Most zoning regulations and building codes were originally intended to protect the public, not to cause trouble. However, be-

cause these codes must apply to everyone in general, they often don't fit your individual situation. Some inspectors see everything "by the book" and are insensitive to the actual circumstances. If you find yourself being instructed to meet requirements that have no practical value, it is perfectly OK to resist—in a friendly, firm, and nonbelligerent way. Just stick to the practical side of the issue. What is the code designed to prevent? Does that situation exist here? If so, how else can it be remedied? When the building inspector demanded that Deanna surround the hot tub on her deck with a high fence that would have cut off the spectacular view that makes living in her house so special, she pointed out that the deck itself gave no access to a child that was so small it would drown in four feet of water. When the inspector insisted that a hypothetical toddler could climb the long and steep driveway, get into the house, find its way out onto the deck, and fall in the tub, she pointed out that the enormous wooden cover on the tub was too heavy for a child to lift—and brought in a couple of kids to prove it. The result was no fence, just a latch for the lid. It took some negotiating, but by being indefatigably cheerful and firmly insisting that she was open to any alternative they might present, she finally won the Building Department over to her side, saving hundreds of dollars and a million dollar view.

6. *Don't be afraid to fight City Hall.* If you want to do something out of the ordinary, or counter to the existing building codes—and there is no reason to belive that it would be unsafe or an eyesore—by all means pursue the project. Every building and zoning agency has a process that allows it to modify its restrictions. Of course, you will have to be willing to undertake a series of extra tasks, such as writing descriptions of, and justifications for,

your project; attending modification hearings; undergoing inspections; and paying various fees for the privilege. Try not to set time limits on the project, if you can. The wheels of state grind slowly, and it may take some time to get the necessary documentation together and run through the mill. Just relax, be patient, and don't panic. If things get rough, don't hesitate to bring in professional and legal help. And remember, if you succeed in setting a new precedent, or in getting an obstructive or unjust restriction set aside, you will have done a service for a lot of other people who would have run into the same problem in the future.

In our city, a woman who wanted to turn her beautiful Spanish mansion into a group household won a landmark case by overturning a law that made it illegal for more than five people to live together if they were not related by blood. In a series of court proceedings, she pointed out that the more than twenty rooms in the house and the acreage on which it sat were more than adequate to house a larger number of people comfortably. She also emphasized that birth and marriage are not the only reasons for living with other people and that it was unfair to bring "blood" into any ruling. She pointed out that housing is both scarce and expensive in our city and that many people who might not otherwise be able to find adequate living space could be accommodated in the larger mansions that had been sitting idle because so few people had the money to rent or buy them, let alone to furnish them. Because of her determination, this woman accomplished not only her own ends, but benefited many other people who now share living space economically because of what she achieved.

The Legal Aspects of Buying or Building a Home Together

This section is for those of you who are thinking of join-
ing forces with other people in order to buy or build a
home together. Since it deals with the dry, legal back
alleys and pitfalls involved, we suggest that everyone
who has no such plans should leap gaily past it to "Settling Conflicts Amicably" (page 200) and get on with the
rest of the chapter. The rest of you "young pioneers" had
better plow through this part. If you know what is involved before you enter a complex situation, you'll have
the best chance of avoiding trouble; and if you do become entangled in legal red tape, you'll be better
equipped to find your way out.

As you may remember, in Chapter I we talked about
the Millers and the Jasons, two young couples who
bought and renovated an old Victorian house so they
could live in it together. Because the high cost of housing
has caused a growing number of people to consider such
joint ventures, legal precedents for handling these arrangements have already been established. However,
because this type of thing is relatively new, many attorneys have had no experience in this area. We visited an
attorney who has handled several such joint purchases,
and he pointed out that to be truly competent, your lawyer should not only be familiar with real estate law, but
with partnership law and family law as well. If you are
lucky, your real estate agent may know of an attorney
who has handled a similar case. If not, try to find a lawyer
who practices partnership and family law and who is
willing and able to get a great deal of input from a real
estate agent who has some experience with people buying homes in tandem. Since there is a growing trend for

unrelated people to buy homes together, many real estate agents have had to become familiar with the legal aspects of the situation.

Because real estate and partnership laws vary greatly from state to state, it would be impossible for us to go into details that would fit even the majority of cases. Instead, we've decided to provide you with a list of things to think about and to consult your attorney and real estate agent about before you sign anything.

Would You Rather Be Co-owners or Partners?

When buying or building a house together, you can either sign co-ownership papers or form a legal partnership. The pros and cons differ from one state to another, so investigate the laws that apply in your state to determine which arrangement will work best for you.

Joint Tenancy Versus Tenancy in Common

These are alternative ways of owning property together. Joint tenancy means that if one of the joint owners dies, the other(s) automatically inherit title to the property. Under tenancy in common, if one of the owners dies, their share of the property goes to their chosen heirs.

Partition Laws

Let's say you buy a home with another person, and after a couple of years that person wants to leave town, or to sell the house for some other reason. Can they force you to sell the house? Partition laws come under the code of civil procedure. They deal with whether one partner can force the sale of co-owned property. What are the procedures for this in your state? Is there any way around them? How can you make sure that you will be in the best position if such a situation arises?

Rights of First Refusal

If one of your partners decides to sell out, or dies, will the rest of you have the right of first refusal to buy his or her portion of the property? If so, are there any monetary limits to determine a fair price? This is a particularly thorny issue if there are several partners—or their heirs—involved. You need to spell things out very carefully here. Be sure to have a formal buy-out agreement drawn up. Some people agree to set a time limit on the home partnership. They agree to sell the property at a specified date, with the option to change this arrangement and keep the place if everyone wants to do so.

Evaluating Your Property

If and when it comes time to sell the property, what will happen if the partners cannot agree upon the value of the house? Usually, everyone formally agrees up front that one or more professional appraisers will be consulted when it is time to determine market value.

Covenant Running with the Land Versus Equitable Servitude

Real estate rights and/or restrictions fit into one of these two categories. A covenant is a promise to do or not to do a particular thing on or with a particular piece of land.

Therefore, covenants are said to "run with the land," which means that even if the property is sold, the covenant will still be in effect. Equitable servitude, on the other hand, deals with a person's rights with respect to property and would therefore terminate when the person in question was no longer the owner of the property.

To give you a practical example: If Joe French and Della Black were to buy a home together, and Joe was terrified of dogs, he might want Della to sign a covenant promising never to keep dogs on the property. Since a covenant runs with the land, if Della sold her share of the house, anyone who bought her share of the property would not be able to keep dogs either. For that matter, if Della and Joe both decided to unload the place altogether, anyone who bought it would be prevented from keeping dogs. This situation might make selling more difficult in the future. However, if under equitable servitude Joe was given the right to prevent dog-keeping on the property, it would keep him secure and still make it possible for a dog lover to move in if and when Joe moved out.

Payments

Be sure to decide specifically how much each of you will pay against the mortgage, balloon payments, property taxes, dues, or assessments. Are you going to split everything down the middle? Prorate it according to the amount of space each partner will use in the building? Or according to the amount of cash or effort each of you has put into the project? Not only that, how will these payments actually be made? Some people simply set up a joint checking account into which each partner pays his or her share of the money owed. Then checks are drawn to make the payments. Whatever you do, keep careful records of collections and disbursals.

Property Maintenance

We're not talking about household chores here, but about major expenditures to repair the property you own in common and to keep it in good condition. If the pipes blow or the roof caves in, who will pay for it? And how? What about painting the place in a couple of years, or resurfacing the driveway? It's best to determine the way you will deal with these things before they happen. You can each put your fair share of cash into a "rainy day" account ahead of time, or simply decide what percentage of such repairs each partner will be responsible for when they become necessary. Some people buy a home warranty insurance policy that covers unusual repairs.

Capital Improvements

It is fairly easy to determine how much each partner will be responsible for when it comes to things that everyone needs (like plumbing repairs and roofing). It is more difficult when one partner wants to add an improvement to the property that the other(s) are not particularly enthusiastic about. If one of you wants to install a Jacuzzi or add an extra bedroom, should everyone have to chip in to pay for it? And if the partner who wants the improvement is willing to bear all the costs, does he or she need the consent of the other partners to go ahead with the project? Consider this: If only one partner pays for an improvement, how should any profits or costs generated by the project be split? After all, it will add to the value of the property, if and when the property is sold—but it will add to the property tax assessment, too.

Further Encumbrances

A piece of real estate is excellent collateral for a loan. Will your partners have the right to take out loans and secure them by a lien on your joint property without everyone's consent? If they default, will you all lose your property? Be sure you spell out each partner's rights, duties, and obligations in this very vital area.

SETTLING CONFLICTS AMICABLY

As we've said before, sharing a home with other people is a lot like a marriage, and it is foolish to go into either situation with unrealistic expectations. No matter how much you like the people you plan to live with, and no matter how well you've always gotten along, you must expect to disagree occasionally—especially when crises occur suddenly.

Whether or not you buy together, build together, rent together, or just live together, there may be times when it is impossible to reach agreement on an important issue. Because of this, many people formally agree up front to seek arbitration or mediation services as an initial means of settling disputes—instead of going to the expense and hassle of hiring attorneys and plowing your way through lengthy and frustrating court procedures. These services are available in most communities and can save everyone concerned a great deal of time and money. If you like, you can place limitations and exceptions on the instances when you will use such services. Of course, being very careful in choosing housemates and partners, spelling out your agreements in detail beforehand, and learning to express your feelings and communicate with one another will do much to avoid having

to resort to professionals of any kind when disagreements arise.

  We've talked elsewhere about leases, security deposits and household agreements, and you might save some
time and money by having your lawyer take a look at all
of these things at once. Although we've tried to provide
you with the tools to evaluate potential housemates and
to promote harmony in living together, the hard truth is
that situations may arise that will make it important to
protect yourself legally from a housemate who turns out
to be a flake. Even if all of your housemates are wonderful people to live with, a written agreement can help
you all to avoid conflicts over just what you agreed to in
the first place.

CULLING OUT THE BAD APPLES

We've tried to provide you with the tools to evaluate
potential housemates properly and to promote harmony
in living together. But sometimes things just don't work
out, and incompatible members of the household must
be asked to leave. Usually, they are no happier than you
are and will be as eager to terminate the arrangement.
However, if you do need to evict tenants or housemates,
there are a few things you should be aware of. The first
is that even if housemates (or *any* tenants, for that matter)
are in violation of a written lease, if they refuse to leave,
you cannot forcibly put them or their belongings out of
the house until you have gone to court, gotten a written
court order, and served them with the proper notice.
Again, the rules of the game will depend on the locality
you live in. When the big day arrives, if they still refuse
to quit the premises, you will have to have a marshal
there to oversee the matter before you can touch a stick

of their furniture. And this is probably just as well, since tempers may rise in the heat of the moment. Hopefully, this situation will never occur, but in the unlikely event that it does, do remember to keep your cool and let the marshal take care of the proceedings.

The Other Side of the Coin

If you are renting space in someone else's home or if your group is renting an apartment or house from someone who does not live there, you also need to think about protecting yourself legally. Contracts and lease agreements should protect all the people involved—both owners and renters. So if the person who owns the place doesn't insist on getting the basic agreements down in writing, be sure that you do—even if it's just handwritten on a piece of stationery. And be sure that everyone involved gets a copy.

When Money Can't Buy Everything

If you choose to share your home with someone who will pay for his or her share of the living expenses in services, rather than money, it may be wise to agree *in writing* just what those services will be and what he or she can expect in return, to avoid hassles later on.

Insurance—Covering Aunt Addie's Chair with More Than an Antimacassar

If you are a homeowner, be sure you have liability insurance that will cover you in case of accidents. What happens if the garage door falls off and bonks someone on the head? Or if the house burns down and ruins not only all of your personal belongings but other peoples' stuff, too? Will your insurance cover these catastrophes? If not, what are your potential liabilities in the matter? If you are renting rooms to others, be sure to add the cost of your home insurance to the other expenses that must be covered by your housemates' monthly payments.

The law is very vague, in fact downright confusing, on matters of liability for the safety of others. In many states, the law distinguishes between "invitees" and "licensees" when dealing with the presence of others on your property. Invitees are people you invite onto your property to conduct business for your economic advantage. In some cases, renters may be considered as falling under this category. On the other hand, licensees are people like milkmen, meter men, etc., who have access to your property to conduct *their* business. Social guests, friends, and relatives are also considered to be licensees under the law. The law imposes a special duty on you to make your premises safe for an invitee, but it only imposes a duty of "reasonable care" toward licensees, who presumably choose to come there at their own risk.

Some of this confusion has been eliminated in California and a few other states, which simply require that you do whatever is "fair and reasonable" to ensure the safety of others on your property. And this is really the key anywhere: In order to sue you for damages, a person has to prove that his or her injury or loss was due to *negligence* on your part. So if you take basic precautions you should be in the clear if accidents occur. To this end, be sure not to leave gaping holes unfilled, make sure walkways are well lit, and don't let old newspapers pile up in the garage near the hot water heater. Get rid of oily rags and empty gasoline cans (the gas fumes are explosive). Don't store flammable materials if you can help it, and if you must, be sure the containers are well vented. Redo surfaces that get slippery in wet weather, and generally keep an eye out for potential hazards and fix them promptly.

No matter how many precautions you take, if you are going to rent out part of your home to strangers, you should make sure you have the best insurance coverage available. This is especially true if you or any of your housemates plan to run any kind of business out of your home (assuming that this is allowable under your local zoning regulations). A home computer that is used to play games, to keep household files, or as a hobby is usually covered by basic home insurance. If you use it to write business letters or a book, or to catch up on work you bring home from the office, you will have to get special coverage for it. If you are taking any part of your home expenses off your taxes as business expenses, be sure to consult your insurance agent to be sure you are covered properly.

If you rent to people with small children, be extra sure that no conditions exist that would be hazardous to kids. Staircases can be a problem, unless you buy a portable gate that can be erected to keep a toddler off the steps. Pools should be fenced off and hot tubs covered to keep the heat in and the kids out. Frankly, if hazardous conditions exist on your property, it might be wiser not to rent to families with small children at all. If accidents occur, the question will be raised, Is it negligent to have a small child on unsafe premises? Even if the parents agree beforehand to take full responsibility, it may make little or no difference in a court of law, should tragedy occur.

Happily, it is possible for you and your housemates to set some limits to liability, providing that you do it in writing, beforehand. If you do this, consult an attorney to be sure that what you've agreed to meets legal precedents.

A lot of people don't realize that they can buy renters' insurance to cover their personal belongings. The fees are nominal when you compare them to the cost of replacing your clothing, books, records, television, stereo, or home computer after a fire, theft, or other disaster. Some insurance will pay the full cost of replacing the article with a new one, other policies only provide coverage prorated by the age of the article. Surprisingly, the full replacement policies are not that much more expensive than the prorated ones. And since Aunt Addie's chair may be quite old, you'd probably want to insure it for full replacement value. Of course, a new chair can never replace Aunt Addie's in your heart, but it will help to have a couple of hundred dollars rather than $4.60 to help you get over your loss.

If you are renting a house as a group, some insurance companies will write a group renters' policy for less than you would have to pay for multiple individual policies. This is certainly worth looking into.

If you buy or build a house with other people, decide in advance on what kind of coverage you want for fire, theft, liability, and other insurance on the property. You might also want mortgage insurance for each of the partners involved to pay off their share of the mortgage if they should become disabled or die.

On this happy note, let's leave this chapter and talk about less drastic endings to your relationships with your housemates. In the next and final chapter, we'll discuss the ways in which you can terminate your group household, or say good-bye to an individual housemate, and manage to remain on the best of terms with everybody concerned.

CHAPTER X

"So Long, It's Been Good to Know You!"

Well, all good things must come to an end, and the chances are that members of your group household will choose to move on as time goes on—and someday, you may choose to do the same.

People decide to move for many reasons: They get married, get transferred, get too rich or too poor to live in the neighborhood—and some of them just get angry and leave. Whatever the circumstances, splitting up is always an event that the psychologists tend to score highly on their stress ratings. By anticipating the inevitable, we hope to help you to lighten the load and make this time of transition as tranquil as possible.

PREVENTIVE MEDICINE TO TAKE THE PAIN OUT OF PARTING

We've already mentioned several things you can do ahead of time to take the hassle out of any leavetaking. It's hard enough to pack up and move from one home to another when you only have your own belongings to consider. If you have to separate them from the communal clutter in a group household, this chore not only becomes more complicated, but it can cause disputes that could set even the most passionately devoted roommates at each other's throats. So do take our advice seriously when it comes to labeling your books, tapes, records, appliances, and kitchen tools (or keeping a written list of who owns what) *as soon as each person moves into the house.* We're not talking about things that stay snug in an individual's room and are only kept for personal use. But everything else that is used communally (or washed communally, if you tend to pool laundry to keep energy costs down) should be labeled or listed. You may feel that you would know your own possessions anywhere, but after listening to a favorite tape or using a particular carving knife for years, it is easy to believe that you brought it into the house in the first place. Take it from us, we have never split up a household without some dispute over who owned what, and it's really hard to settle these issues fairly.

OK. That takes care of personal possessions. But what about things that were bought communally—or maintained communally? We've already discussed the problem of furniture and appliances that have been purchased communally in chapter III, and since it is a relatively complicated issue, we suggest that you go back and read it if you've lost the message in the wealth of fascinating data we've thrown at you since then. Again, we strongly suggest that you all agree on how these items will be disposed of, *before* you pool your money to buy them.

AVOIDING CUSTODY BATTLES

Consider this: If you paid $2.00 for a teeny little houseplant a couple of years ago and one of your roommates has lavished water, fish emulsion, and love on it ever since—and maybe bought it a larger pot and a bag of potting soil, too—just who does that plant really belong to? Or if one member of your household rescued a baby puppy from the pound, and everyone in the house has walked it, fed it, bathed it, and adored it for years, who's dog is it? These can be thorny emotional issues when someone is leaving the household and wants to take the little darling along.

How do you award custody of the critter fairly? There are no hard and fast rules, but we tend to feel that for animals or plants it is much more a matter of parenting than ownership. So if one person has been responsible for caring for a living thing, then that person keeps it, no matter who originally brought it into the house. And if everyone has taken part in the parenting, then the plant or animal belongs to the house and stays there until the household breaks up completely. At that point you can draw straws to see who the lucky owner will be if the problem can't be resolved easily. So if you bring a live creature into a group household, either see to it that you do the work involved in caring for it or be prepared to acknowledge that one or all of your roommates have become the "real parents" over time. Note, however, that all of the above usually does not apply to children. No matter how much attention they've received from your roommates, blood is thicker than chocolate milk!

"I Love You, I Hate You, Good-Bye!"

Even if you have no ownership problems with plants, pets, tots, or television sets, little things can assume enormous proportions when a roommate is leaving the household. Although everyone concerned may be parting on the best of terms and for the most favorable of reasons, there may still be a feeling of rejection for those who are being left behind—and a feeling of estrangement for the one who is leaving the rest of the "family." As a result, emotions tend to get confused, and some really weird things can happen. Here's a case in point:

Sam Franco owns his own home and has run it as a group household for many years. Sam is a really nice guy: intelligent, easygoing, unchauvinistic, generous, and fair-minded. Most of his housemates find him a wonderful person to live with—until they decide to move out. Then he turns into a totally different person: picky, stingy, snide and cutting. He sneaks and spies on everything his outgoing roommate packs—and everything the poor soul eats or uses until moving day arrives. He suddenly becomes convinced that he is being robbed and will claim previously uncontested possessions as his own. Over the years this pattern has been repeated again and again. It is as though having someone move out of his house sends this usually well-adjusted individual out of his mind. It doesn't matter whether the parting starts out amicably or otherwise, it always ends up miserably for everyone concerned.

Recently, Betty Douglas, who had lived in Sam's home for some years and watched this scene repeated several times, decided to move into her boy friend's apartment so they could see whether they were compatible enough to be married. Betty was determined to keep the parting with Sam amicable. They had become close friends over the years, and that friendship mattered a great deal to her. Besides, if living with her boy friend didn't work out, she wanted to be able to move back into Sam's house, if possible. So, even though he seemed delighted that her love life was prospering, assured her that he would have no trouble in renting her room, and had nothing but positive feelings about the entire situation, she felt that it was important for her to tell Sam what she had observed and to ask him, "What is going on here and how can it be prevented?" Sam was willing to admit that he had gone through periods of pain when someone moved out of his household. He decided to ask a friend of his who was a psychologist about it. After some deliberation they came up with answers that could apply to many people in similar situations.

Sam's folks divorced when he was quite young, and from what he remembers, it was one of those classic horror stories. After much anger and grief, his father left home, and for years afterward Sam's mother constantly repeated her heartbreaking story about how his dad had ripped them off and left them alone and penniless "with scarcely a roof over our heads or food in our bellies." It doesn't really matter whether things were really that bad—or whether Sam's dad had any other alternatives. Sam and his mom survived, but the terror of being abandoned and "left to starve" remained with him. As he matured and prospered, those memories were buried and forgotten. Except that whenever someone prepared to leave Sam's household that little child who lay buried deep within his consciousness awoke, terrified that the entire scenario would be repeated. Sam was unaware of this, and the result was that he looked for "reasonable" things on which to blame his irrational feelings of fear and loss. Consequently, he transferred all the suspicion and anger he had learned from his mother's tirades to his outgoing roommates.

Once she understood these dynamics, Betty decided that during the final weeks of her stay in Sam's house she would make a very special effort to spend time with him as often as possible and to reassure him that their friendship would continue. She also asked him if he would undertake some carpentry projects in her new home and made sure he knew he was invited to a party she was going to hold after she had moved. Betty was very open and honest about how much she had liked living with Sam and how much she hated to leave his house. In addition, she did her best to encourage him to express his feelings about her leaving.

When it came time to pack, she asked for his assistance and went out of her way to avoid taking anything they'd acquired together. As a result, it was Sam who felt free to remind her that she had chipped in to buy the new set of glassware and was entitled to take some of it with her (she declined), and who insisted that she take the extensive collection of spices she'd built up in the pantry. "You're the only one who knows what to do with them," he assured her. "I'd rather get invited over to your house to eat them than watch them turn to dust over here."

By staying in close touch all during those difficult days, Betty helped Sam to avoid feeling like an abandoned little boy. Consequently, they remain the best of friends to this day.

Now, what has this story to do with you? It simply serves to illustrate, in a somewhat melodramatic way, the strange emotions that may arise when a good friend and housemate chooses to leave your extended family. If such emotions begin to arise for you or for other people in your household when moving day approaches, you might want to check out what is going on beneath the surface.

"Parting Is Such Sweet Sorrow!"

Sometimes the situation may be reversed and the one who is leaving the household may experience feelings of grief and loss:

Patsy, Cleo, and Monica had been roommates in college. When they graduated, they decided to move to New York City to seek their fortunes, and it seemed only natural for them to find a large apartment to share. For the next three years, as each one struggled to gain a foothold in her chosen field, they were able to provide each other with the understanding and support that makes "comrades in arms" the tightest kind of friends. Men came and went in each of their lives, but the roommates agreed that, for a while at least, their careers came first. Then, Cleo fell in love.

At first, it seemed as though Stan was just another "man of the hour" who would be a frequent visitor and then an overnight guest until the affair had run its course. But Stan hung right in there, and as the months passed it became obvious that he was in Cleo's life to stay. Neither Patsy nor Monica minded having him around the house, but as Stan pointed out on the night he proposed marriage, "Married people usually have a place of their own to live in. It goes with the territory." So Cleo began to make plans to move into Stan's apartment. When she first broached the subject to her roommates, they were delighted that she was going to be married. Naturally, they were also a bit sad at the thought of living without her, but they soon recovered and began to look for someone to rent Cleo's room.

Then, to everyone's amazement, as the final month of her stay in the house wore on, Cleo began to act less like a Cinderella who had found her Handsome Prince—and more like one of the Wicked Stepsisters. Although she had always been the best housekeeper in the apartment, she suddenly began to leave her things all over the living room and to abandon her kitchen and bathroom duties completely. Weeks before she even began to pack, her room became a wilderness of possessions and boxes.

When her roommates interviewed prospective housemates, she was cutting and surly, and seemed to suggest
to the bewildered applicants that they "didn't know what
they were getting into." Patsy and Monica were mysti-
fied and quite a bit upset. Finally, they tackled "Ms.
Hyde" at a family meeting.

Patsy, who was feeling very angry at Cleo, tried to
conceal her hostility under the guise of sympathetic understanding. "Listen Cleo," she said, "we realize that
getting married is kind of a heavy thing to be going
through. But if the thought of it is upsetting you so much,
maybe you ought to think it over."

Cleo looked at her in amazement. "What are you talking about? I have no problems with getting married, I
can hardly wait for the wedding. I really love Stan."

Monica patted her hand sympathetically. "We know
you do, honey, but you've been so uptight lately, we felt
that you might be having second thoughts." As Cleo continued to look blank, she added, "You know we love you
and we want you to be happy. If there's anything you
need to talk over, we'd be happy to hear you out."

"But I am happy!" Cleo assured her. "Whatever gave
you the idea that I wasn't?"

"Well," Monica responded, as diplomatically as possible, "you have been a bit . . . strange . . . lately."

Patsy could contain herself no longer; she had never
been one to mince words. "You've been behaving like
a total bitch! You act as though you hate us, and you've
been making a pigsty out of this place, just when we're
trying to convince some unsuspecting stranger that we'd
be wonderful to live with!"

There was a moment of silence before Cleo (who had
gone from shock to anger to understanding in about as
many seconds as it takes to say those words) managed to
reply. "You're right," she said in a tiny voice, scarcely

looking at her roommates, who sat there feeling just as miserable as she did. "I have been a bitch . . . and a slob, too. I could see myself doing it, but I just couldn't seem to control it. Oh, I'm terribly sorry"—her words came out in a rush—"I love you guys so much and the last thing I wanted was for you to be angry at me!"

The three of them devoted the next few minutes to hugging and tear-blotting and other reassuring gestures. When their emotions subsided, they all settled down to deal with the situation.

"We've been so close for so long," Cleo continued when she had found her voice again. "We've practically grown up together over the past seven years—closer than sisters—and now all that is going to be over. Sometimes I think I just can't handle moving out. But then, that seems silly. I mean, I would be crazy not to marry Stan because I can't bear to leave my roommates!"

Monica put her arm around Cleo and drew her down next to her on the couch. "Why should you feel that our closeness will end? I'll never stop being your friend and neither will Patsy. The three of us will always feel like sisters, no matter where we live."

"Besides," said practical Patsy, "neither Monica nor I plan to be old maids. Someday we'll get married and then you'd end up here alone. You might as well leave now, girl. Someone has to be first!"

They were all laughing by then, and it made it easier for Cleo to continue her confession. "I know it's foolish, but I think of you two staying on together here, and I feel left out. And—please don't think I'm silly—I feel jealous of the new roommate who's going to take my place. I find myself wondering if you'll like her better than you liked me!" She got up and crossed the room, unable to bear their sympathetic scrutiny. "It's all so childish, I can't believe I'm actually saying these absurd things, but you wanted to know what's been going inside me . . . and that's why I've been acting so rotten lately."

To Cleo's delight, Patsy and Monica really understood. It only took a minute for each of them to put herself into Cleo's place and see how she would feel under the same circumstances. After that, none of them needed any further convincing that they would all continue to be friends "to the end." They made plans to get together every week "just like old times." As Patsy pointed out, "Every bride needs to get the hell out of the house sometimes, and spend an evening out with 'the girls.' Otherwise she'd probably go mad and strangle her husband!"

"And even when we can't get together, we'll only be a telephone call away, no matter what time it is," said Monica reassuringly.

Patsy nodded in wry agreement. "Sure, you can find us chained to our desks from morning till dusk, and busy making lace for our hope chests every evening."

"Of course, you must come to visit me at home sometimes, so I can do my happy-homemaker routines for you," Cleo reminded them loftily. "Do bring 'the new girl' along occasionally, won't you?" she continued in her best high-society voice. "I wouldn't want her to feel left out!"

The evening ended on a note of general hilarity and the rest of the month went smoothly. Although the promised weekly get-togethers soon began to occur less frequently because of the busy social and work schedules that mark happy and successful lives, the three have remained close friends and probably will continue to do so. As the irrepressible Patsy once put it, "Roommates and lovers may come and go, but we three will probably live happily ever after—although not necessarily together."

"PLEASE DON'T TALK ABOUT ME WHEN I'M GONE!"

Even if a roommate's departure is unmarred by any emotional upheavals or quarrels over possessions, there are still a couple of problems that may arise *after* a roommate has moved out of the house. And the fact that the individual is no longer on the scene makes these problems even more difficult to resolve. Once again, the wisest thing to do is to take preventive measures beforehand. Please note that when we say "beforehand" we do not mean before a housemate is ready to depart. These troubleshooting techniques must be put into action as soon as each roommate joins the household.

Money Can't Buy Friendship—But It Sure Can Help One Last!

Your dear roommate Fred is leaving town. He's been a wonderful person to live with, and although you won't be seeing much of him, it's important to all of you that you remain friends for a long time to come. It would be a pity if something as mundane as money came between you and drove you apart forever. However, when someone leaves home, it is not uncommon for unpaid bills and unfulfilled obligations (or unanticipated expectations) to rear their ugly heads and destroy a relationship that might have brought years of pleasure to all concerned. If Fred is leaving on the last day of June, there is no way of telling how much he will owe toward the June utility bills until he is long gone. Therefore, as we've indicated in the Household Agreement in chapter VIII, be sure to collect both first and last month's rent, plus a cleaning and security deposit from each new member of your household, *before he or she moves in.* Now, we realize that this can amount to a considerable sum of money, but as you, no doubt, are painfully aware, it is common practice in most rental situations to demand these financial safeguards. On the positive side, the fact that Fred has already paid that last month's rent in advance will be a blessing when it comes time for him to move out, because it means that he can use the money he would have owed for the last month's rent on his old lodgings to pay the advance deposits on his new residence.

Fred's security and cleaning deposit should be used to pay his outstanding June utility bills, when they arrive. Otherwise, you will have to delay payment (and risk incurring late-payment charges) until you can locate him to tell him how much he owes. Even then, he will probably have to mail you a check, the post office will have to deliver it, and you will have to cash it, before you can pay those bills. Or the other members of your household (or you alone, if you are the landlord) will have to ante up Fred's share of the money in order to pay the bills on time. Although good old Fred will probably pay up eventually, this all seems unnecessarily risky and complicated when all you need to do is to use Fred's deposit to pay his share of the bills.

Once the bills have been paid, the rest of Fred's security and cleaning deposit should be returned to him immediately—unless he has neglected to leave his room in habitable condition. All those who choose to become members of a group household should understand that when they decide to move on they will be expected to leave the place in good shape for their successors. If Fred folds his tents and quietly steals away, leaving his room in a state of filth and disrepair, then the balance of his deposit will have to go toward cleaning, painting, and repairing the damage.

Please be aware that this does *not* give you carte blanche to spend Fred's cleaning and security deposit in any way you wish. It is only fair to give him plenty of time to satisfy any complaints you may have regarding the condition of his room well before those last hectic moving days arrive. It would be cruel to inform him, as he is on his way out of the door, that he has to paint the place or repair the built-ins or you will have to use his money to hire someone else to do it. Therefore, as soon he gives notice that he is planning to move, he should be reminded of his obligation to leave the place in good condition, and an agreement should be reached as to what he will be expected to do to restore things to order before he moves out. Then if he sneaks out like a slob anyway, you will be justified in using the balance of his deposit to make whatever repairs you'd agreed upon— and nothing more.

Because most rental periods begin and end on the first and last days of the month, in many cases rooms change hands within twenty-four hours. Avoid this if you can. Building in a day or two between departures and arrivals will give everyone concerned a chance to deal with the unexpected and will considerably lessen the chaos and tension for the other members of your household. There is no way that Fred can leave his room clean if someone else is moving stuff into it at precisely the same time as he is trying to vacate the premises. Besides, if the room has to be repainted, it would be nice if the paint had a chance to dry—and the paint smell to subside—before your new housemate moves in.

When moving day arrives, try to be there to lend Fred a helping hand—and to be sure that he leaves the room in good shape. He may normally be a good and trustworthy fellow, but even the best intentions can go awry when the pressure is on.

Once the utility bills have been paid and everything is in order, be sure to send Fred the balance of his deposit immediately. Unless truly extraordinary circumstances arise to prevent it, all cleanup and repairs should be made and the whole matter settled before the end of the month. Be sure to send Fred copies of all the bills you used his money to pay, along with his check. It's nice to know where your money went, especially when someone else is spending it!

"I Never Want to Speak to You Again—But Be Sure to Keep in Touch!"

Roommates may leave, but their mail and phone messages seem to go on and on forever. For this reason, it is very important to obtain a forwarding address and a telephone number from every outgoing housemate, before he or she leaves the house. If someone is going on the road and has no idea of where he or she will end up, at least encourage the departing housemember to consider getting a P.O. box, an answering service, or permission to forward calls and mail to a friend or relative. Although a housemate may have left your group household on the best of terms, no matter how well-intentioned and conscientious the rest of the household is about gathering and forwarding stuff to the "dear departed," if things must lie around until the wandering one calls for them, they will tend to get forgotten or lost in the shuffle. And if there are three or more individuals in your household, it will be quite enough for everyone to keep track of the incoming mail and phone calls for the current members, without having to ride herd on messages for a backlog of departed roommates.

How to Make the Post Office Work for You

It is a relatively easy matter to arrange for the post office to forward mail—and they are usually willing to do it for an entire year. They are also willing to help you inform everyone who sends you mail or calls you of your change of address. Because we've found many otherwise well-informed people who have no idea that such services are offered, or how to go about obtaining them, we've decided to tell you exactly what to do so you'll know what to look for.

First, as soon as you know your new address, go down to the Post Office and tell them that you are moving. They will give you a card to fill out with your old address, your new address, the date you are moving, and the types of mail you would like them to forward. If you have been up to your ears in junk mail, the good news is that they normally won't forward anything but first-class mail and "parcels of obvious value." However, you may also agree to pay forwarding postage for newspapers and magazines for ninety days, which should give the subscription departments a chance to change their records and catch up with you. Since all kinds of public services are currently being cut back, we would advise that you check with your Post Office when you are ready to move to find out just how long they will continue to forward your mail automatically. If you are still getting important mail addressed to your former abode after the forwarding period has expired, you will have to repeat this process at your former Post Office or they will stop forwarding the stuff to you.

The Post Office also provides change of address cards that you can use to inform everyone who might want to get in touch with you that you are moving. Because it makes their job easier, they provide these free of charge and will give you as many as you want. You will need quite a few, so don't be bashful about loading up on them. If you take too many, you can always return the ones you don't use. Although the cards are free, you will have to pay postage to send them—but they are well worth the expense and the time it takes to fill them out. Here is a list of places to be sure to send them to:

Your family and friends
Your kid's pen pals
Your bank and other financial agencies
Your insurance companies
Your alma mater and alumni association
Any charities or causes you regularly support—especially the ones who send publications to their supporters
Every periodical you subscribe to
Any business acquaintances who regularly write or call you at home
Financial credit cards you hold, such as Visa and Master Charge
Any stores where you have charge accounts
The gasoline companies whose credit cards you use
Your church and other affiliations
The registrar's office and/or the attendance office, if you or your children currently attend school
Your doctor, dentist, lawyer, accountant, shrink, etc.

To make this task more efficient, go through your address book and keep a stack of these cards on your desk so you can fill them out as the mail comes in from places you've forgotten to notify. Try to get started on this as soon as you know the address you'll be moving to. Once moving day arrives, you'll have more than enough to keep you occupied. It is especially important to inform the subscription departments of periodicals well in advance, since it takes them up to six weeks to make the changes on their mailing lists.

How to Get the Best Out of Your Local Phone Company

If you are able to find out what your new phone number will be in time to include it on your change-of-address cards, you will be able to save yourself a great deal of inconvenience. It is often possible to have the phone company reserve a telephone number for you weeks before you are ready to begin service. This is not the sort of thing they are thrilled about doing, but if you have a nice friendly chat with the highest-ranking supervisor available, you probably will be able to bring it off. Explain that it is vitally important that you be able to notify business or professional contacts well in advance of your move—or give them a better story, if you have one.

It really pays to order your new telephone very far in advance. It may be hard to believe in these days of advanced telecommunications and satellite systems, but in some localities people have recently had to wait from three weeks to more than a month before they were able to obtain service. Sometimes this is because the local phone company is shorthanded and far behind on service calls. In other places, there is a shortage of new lines and you have to wait until a number becomes free. Therefore, get in touch with the phone company as soon as you know your new address, even if you are not planning to move for more than a month.

In some cases, if there is already a line and a phone jack on the premises, the phone company will be able to open the line from their offices without sending out a service truck, provided you already have a phone you can plug in yourself. This is one of the many reasons why it pays to own your own telephone equipment these days. You can buy a pushbutton phone that will place a caller on hold and will automatically redial busy numbers, for under $10. If you have been renting a phone from the phone company for $1.25 per month or more, these goodies will pay for themselves in a few months and save you money forever after, even if they don't convey your dulcet tones with quite the fidelity of higher priced gear.

Here's another pitfall to look out for: When the phone company is ready to assign you a new number, be sure to ask them how long that number has been buried and who the last party was who had it. By "buried" we mean out of service—and this can be very important indeed. When Deanna last changed her residence, her new phone began to ring constantly—and the calls were seldom for her. For a writer, a minor interruption can mean an hour of concentration lost, so she called the phone company to find out what was happening. It seemed that her personal phone number had belonged to a couple who had canceled their service only days before hers began. There had been no time for anyone to find out that Bob and Rosie Fairfield had moved. To make matters worse, they had left no forwarding address. Deanna urged everyone who called asking for Bob and Rosie to have the Fairfields call her with their new number. But apparently no one ever found them, including Deanna. To add insult to injury, when the new phonebook came out half a year later and she looked to see if the Fairfields had a new number, Deanna was appalled to find that the phone company had continued to list them with—you guessed it—her number!

Therefore, when she later had a business phone installed, Deanna was a bit wiser. This time, as soon as the first few calls for service came in, and she realized that the new number had belonged to a prominent water purification company, she was wise enough to insist that her number be changed immediately. It was either that or change her name to Culligan.

A Few Final Words

Well, here we are at the end of this book and it's time for us to say good-bye too. We've told you all we know about the joys and tribulations of group housekeeping, and we hope we've convinced you that it is well worth the effort. As we look back on these pages we see that there are an awful lot of do's and don'ts—and what seems like a great many rules and procedures to follow. So please be assured that we don't expect anyone to follow all of them; in fact, we urge you not to. Any household where *all* of these structures and rules were rigidly enforced would not be a friendly or relaxed place to live. We simply want to point out all the situations that might come up and to provide you with ways to deal with them. To give you an idea how simple group housekeeping really can be, this entire book boils down to two sentences:

Absolutely anything goes in a group household —provided everyone agrees to it.
and
Be willing to openly communicate your needs and your feelings to your housemates—and be just as willing to listen to theirs as well.

Since group housekeeping is still a relatively new phenomenon, we consider this book to be a bit of a pioneer in its field. If it motivates you to join forces with other people in a unique living arrangement—or if you encounter and deal with situations we haven't covered in these pages—please get in touch with us through our publishers and share your experiences with us so we can add them to future editions of this book. After all, we pioneers have to stick together!

About The Authors

Teona Tone and *Deanna Sclar* met at a Greyhound bus station. Their ensuing friendship turned collaborative when they combined Teona's idea for a book on shared housekeeping with Deanna's experience with non-fiction writing. The authors drew their material from personal experience and from interviews conducted with family, friends, and a broad range of people encountered in their travels. While each has lived in a number of different kinds of shared housekeeping situations, they have never lived together.

Teona Tone has a Ph.D. in English and American literature, is a former private detective and the author of two Fawcett Gold Medal mystery novels, *Lady on the Line* and *Full Cry.* Deanna Sclar is the author of *Auto Repair for Dummies* (McGraw-Hill), now in its second edition. As consumer spokesperson for two major corporations, her media appearances have made her familiar to do-it-your-selfers all over the country.